Practice Adding, Subtracting, Multiplying, and Dividing Fractions Workbook

Improve Your Math Fluency Series

Chris McMullen, Ph.D.

Practice Adding, Subtracting, Multiplying, and Dividing Fractions Workbook
Improve Your Math Fluency Series

CreateSpace

Nonfiction / Children's Books / Science, Nature, & How It Works / Math / Fractions
Nonfiction / Children's Books / Educational / Study Aids / Test Preparation
Professional & Technical / Education / Specific Skills / Mathematics

ISBN: 1451534701

EAN-13: 9781451534702

Contents

Multiplication Table

	1	2	3	4	5	6	7	8	9	10
1	1	2	3	4	5	6	7	8	9	10
2	2	4	6	8	10	12	14	16	18	20
3	3	6	9	12	15	18	21	24	27	30
4	4	8	12	16	20	24	28	32	36	40
5	5	10	15	20	25	30	35	40	45	50
6	6	12	18	24	30	36	42	48	54	60
7	7	14	21	28	35	42	49	56	63	70
8	8	16	24	32	40	48	56	64	72	80
9	9	18	27	36	45	54	63	72	81	90
10	10	20	30	40	50	60	70	80	90	100

Making the Most of this Workbook

- Mathematics is a language. You can't hold a decent conversation in any language if you have a limited vocabulary or if you are not fluent. In order to become successful in mathematics, you need to practice until you have mastered the fundamentals and developed fluency in the subject. This *Practice Adding, Subtracting, Multiplying, and Dividing Fractions Workbook* will help you improve the fluency with which you add, subtract, multiply, and divide fractions.

- You may need to consult the multiplication table on page 4 occasionally as you begin your practice, but should refrain from relying on it. Force yourself to solve the problems independently as much as possible. It is necessary to memorize the basic multiplication facts and know them quickly in order to become successful at finding a common denominator and reducing your answers.

- This book is conveniently divided into four parts: Part 1 focuses on adding fractions, Part 2 on subtracting fractions, Part 3 on multiplying fractions, and Part 4 on dividing fractions. This way you can focus on one arithmetic operation at a time.

- Each section begins with a concise set of instructions for how to add, subtract, multiply, or divide fractions. These instructions are followed by a couple of examples. Use these examples as a guide until you become fluent in the technique.

- After you complete a page, check your answers with the answer key in the back of the book. Practice makes permanent, but not necessarily perfect: If you practice making mistakes, you will learn your mistakes. Check your answers and learn from your mistakes such that you practice solving the problems correctly. This way your practice will make perfect.

- Math can be fun. Make a game of your practice by recording your times and trying to improve on your times, and recording your scores and trying to improve on your scores. Doing this will help you see how much you are improving, and this sign of improvement can give you the confidence to succeed in math, which can help you learn to enjoy this subject more.

Part 1: Practice Adding Fractions

Two fractions can be added together by first finding a common denominator. You can multiply the denominators together to find a common denominator, but it is often more convenient to find the lowest common denominator. You can find the lowest common denominator by first checking to see if the denominators share a common factor. For example, if one denominator is 4 and the other is 6, the common factor is 2 (i.e. 4 and 6 are each evenly divisible by 2). So although 24 (found by multiplying the 4 and 6 together) would serve as a suitable common denominator, it is more convenient to divide this by the common factor (which was 2) to obtain the lowest common denominator of 12.

Once you have a common denominator, multiply the numerator and denominator of each fraction (separately) by the factor needed to make the common denominator. The same factor must multiply both the numerator and denominator, but a different factor will usually be applied to the different fractions being added together. For example, if adding 3/4 to 1/6, multiply the numerator and denominator of 3/4 by 3 to obtain the lowest common denominator of 12, making the fraction 9/12, and multiply the numerator and denominator of 1/6 by 2, making this fraction 2/12. The two fractions 9/12 and 2/12 have the same common denominator.

Once the denominators are the same, simply add the numerators together. Adding 9/12 and 2/12 together, the result is 11/12.

Sometimes, the answer will be reducible. For example, the fraction 8/12 is reducible. To reduce a fraction, look for the greatest common factor in the numerator and denominator. For the fraction 8/12, the greatest common factor is 4 (i.e. the 8 and 12 are each evenly divisible by 4). Dividing the numerator and denominator each by 4, the fraction 8/12 is reduced to 2/3.

EXAMPLES

$$\frac{2}{3} + \frac{3}{4}$$

$$= \frac{4 \cdot 2}{4 \cdot 3} + \frac{3 \cdot 3}{3 \cdot 4}$$

$$= \frac{8}{12} + \frac{9}{12}$$

$$= \frac{8 + 9}{12}$$

$$= \frac{17}{12}$$

$$\frac{3}{2} + \frac{1}{6}$$

$$= \frac{3 \cdot 3}{3 \cdot 2} + \frac{1}{6}$$

$$= \frac{9}{6} + \frac{1}{6}$$

$$= \frac{10}{6}$$

$$= \frac{5}{3}$$

$\frac{1}{2} + \frac{4}{5}$ $\frac{9}{4} + \frac{5}{3}$ $\frac{1}{3} + \frac{8}{7}$ $\frac{2}{7} + \frac{1}{3}$ $\frac{4}{7} + \frac{1}{6}$

$\frac{1}{6} + \frac{9}{7}$ $\frac{7}{9} + \frac{4}{9}$ $\frac{9}{8} + \frac{1}{2}$ $\frac{4}{3} + \frac{7}{6}$ $\frac{1}{6} + \frac{1}{7}$

$\frac{3}{2} + \frac{8}{5}$ $\frac{3}{5} + \frac{6}{5}$ $\frac{3}{8} + \frac{3}{7}$ $\frac{5}{2} + \frac{7}{3}$ $\frac{7}{8} + \frac{7}{3}$

$\frac{9}{7} + \frac{3}{7}$ $\frac{3}{7} + \frac{9}{7}$ $\frac{5}{2} + \frac{9}{4}$ $\frac{7}{9} + \frac{7}{6}$ $\frac{7}{9} + \frac{7}{9}$

$\frac{4}{9} + \frac{1}{4}$ $\frac{8}{3} + \frac{9}{4}$ $\frac{5}{8} + \frac{4}{7}$ $\frac{6}{7} + \frac{9}{5}$ $\frac{8}{3} + \frac{5}{8}$

$\frac{7}{9} + \frac{5}{3} =$ $\frac{4}{7} + \frac{3}{8} =$ $\frac{1}{4} + \frac{8}{7}$ $\frac{4}{5} + \frac{2}{3}$ $\frac{8}{5} + \frac{3}{8}$

$= \frac{7}{9} + \frac{15}{9} = \frac{22}{9}$

$\frac{3}{8} + \frac{7}{6}$ $\frac{1}{5} + \frac{2}{3}$ $\frac{5}{2} + \frac{5}{4}$ $\frac{3}{5} + \frac{1}{4}$ $\frac{9}{8} + \frac{5}{4}$

$\frac{5}{2} + \frac{2}{3}$ $\frac{2}{9} + \frac{9}{8}$ $\frac{5}{3} + \frac{3}{8}$ $\frac{7}{5} + \frac{1}{4}$ $\frac{3}{2} + \frac{3}{4}$

$\frac{5}{6} + \frac{9}{2}$ $\frac{4}{3} + \frac{9}{2}$ $\frac{3}{2} + \frac{5}{8}$ $\frac{1}{4} + \frac{1}{2}$ $\frac{4}{5} + \frac{3}{5}$

$\frac{3}{8} + \frac{7}{5}$ $\frac{9}{4} + \frac{2}{9}$ $\frac{2}{9} + \frac{2}{3}$ $\frac{9}{4} + \frac{2}{5}$ $\frac{7}{9} + \frac{1}{7}$

$\frac{9}{4} + \frac{8}{7} =$ $\frac{1}{5} + \frac{6}{7}$ $\frac{6}{7} + \frac{8}{3}$ $\frac{3}{5} + \frac{7}{9}$ $\frac{5}{7} + \frac{4}{7}$

$$\frac{63}{28} + \frac{32}{28} = \frac{95}{28}$$

$\frac{9}{7} + \frac{1}{6}$ $\frac{7}{4} + \frac{7}{6}$ $\frac{1}{5} + \frac{1}{7}$ $\frac{2}{7} + \frac{1}{5}$ $\frac{2}{3} + \frac{3}{4}$

$\frac{6}{5} + \frac{6}{5}$ $\frac{8}{7} + \frac{7}{4}$ $\frac{3}{7} + \frac{7}{4}$ $\frac{8}{7} + \frac{8}{3}$ $\frac{2}{5} + \frac{1}{3}$

$\frac{3}{5} + \frac{5}{7}$ $\frac{7}{6} + \frac{7}{6}$ $\frac{1}{6} + \frac{1}{3}$ $\frac{3}{4} + \frac{7}{8}$ $\frac{5}{6} + \frac{8}{9}$

$\frac{1}{2} + \frac{2}{7}$ $\frac{8}{9} + \frac{6}{7}$ $\frac{2}{9} + \frac{5}{9}$ $\frac{8}{9} + \frac{7}{6}$ $\frac{4}{9} + \frac{7}{3}$

$\dfrac{7}{6} + \dfrac{8}{9}$ $\qquad$ $\dfrac{7}{8} + \dfrac{8}{7}$ $\qquad$ $\dfrac{7}{3} + \dfrac{3}{8}$ $\qquad$ $\dfrac{2}{7} + \dfrac{5}{6}$ $\qquad$ $\dfrac{9}{4} + \dfrac{3}{7}$

$\dfrac{9}{5} + \dfrac{9}{7}$ $\qquad$ $\dfrac{5}{9} + \dfrac{2}{9}$ $\qquad$ $\dfrac{2}{9} + \dfrac{7}{6}$ $\qquad$ $\dfrac{7}{6} + \dfrac{2}{5}$ $\qquad$ $\dfrac{6}{7} + \dfrac{5}{2}$

$\dfrac{8}{7} + \dfrac{9}{4}$ $\qquad$ $\dfrac{4}{3} + \dfrac{6}{7}$ $\qquad$ $\dfrac{1}{5} + \dfrac{6}{7}$ $\qquad$ $\dfrac{1}{4} + \dfrac{1}{6}$ $\qquad$ $\dfrac{2}{5} + \dfrac{1}{8}$

$\dfrac{1}{3} + \dfrac{3}{8}$ $\qquad$ $\dfrac{7}{4} + \dfrac{1}{3}$ $\qquad$ $\dfrac{4}{9} + \dfrac{8}{5}$ $\qquad$ $\dfrac{3}{2} + \dfrac{1}{8}$ $\qquad$ $\dfrac{3}{5} + \dfrac{3}{4}$

$\dfrac{7}{2} + \dfrac{4}{9}$ $\qquad$ $\dfrac{5}{2} + \dfrac{5}{4}$ $\qquad$ $\dfrac{7}{9} + \dfrac{3}{4}$ $\qquad$ $\dfrac{9}{2} + \dfrac{8}{3}$ $\qquad$ $\dfrac{8}{3} + \dfrac{5}{2}$

$\dfrac{1}{2} + \dfrac{1}{8}$ $\qquad$ $\dfrac{4}{3} + \dfrac{4}{5}$ $\qquad$ $\dfrac{7}{3} + \dfrac{9}{4}$ $\qquad$ $\dfrac{7}{5} + \dfrac{9}{8}$ $\qquad$ $\dfrac{9}{4} + \dfrac{9}{2}$

$\dfrac{9}{8} + \dfrac{2}{9}$ $\qquad$ $\dfrac{2}{3} + \dfrac{7}{2}$ $\qquad$ $\dfrac{7}{8} + \dfrac{6}{7}$ $\qquad$ $\dfrac{2}{9} + \dfrac{8}{3}$ $\qquad$ $\dfrac{8}{7} + \dfrac{4}{3}$

$\dfrac{2}{3} + \dfrac{5}{2}$ $\qquad$ $\dfrac{1}{5} + \dfrac{9}{4}$ $\qquad$ $\dfrac{2}{3} + \dfrac{6}{5}$ $\qquad$ $\dfrac{4}{3} + \dfrac{7}{2}$ $\qquad$ $\dfrac{1}{7} + \dfrac{5}{2}$

$\dfrac{8}{9} + \dfrac{9}{8}$ $\qquad$ $\dfrac{5}{6} + \dfrac{8}{9}$ $\qquad$ $\dfrac{8}{7} + \dfrac{5}{4}$ $\qquad$ $\dfrac{3}{5} + \dfrac{5}{2}$ $\qquad$ $\dfrac{1}{8} + \dfrac{2}{5}$

$\dfrac{9}{7} + \dfrac{2}{5}$ $\qquad$ $\dfrac{7}{5} + \dfrac{9}{5}$ $\qquad$ $\dfrac{6}{7} + \dfrac{9}{4}$ $\qquad$ $\dfrac{1}{9} + \dfrac{5}{4}$ $\qquad$ $\dfrac{3}{2} + \dfrac{4}{3}$

$\dfrac{2}{5} + \dfrac{1}{4}$ $\dfrac{1}{8} + \dfrac{2}{3}$ $\dfrac{1}{7} + \dfrac{7}{5}$ $\dfrac{7}{5} + \dfrac{9}{8}$ $\dfrac{9}{7} + \dfrac{6}{5}$

$\dfrac{7}{3} + \dfrac{7}{5}$ $\dfrac{8}{7} + \dfrac{8}{9}$ $\dfrac{7}{6} + \dfrac{3}{4}$ $\dfrac{9}{2} + \dfrac{2}{9}$ $\dfrac{9}{7} + \dfrac{1}{3}$

$\dfrac{5}{6} + \dfrac{9}{7}$ $\dfrac{7}{6} + \dfrac{1}{2}$ $\dfrac{7}{5} + \dfrac{7}{5}$ $\dfrac{5}{2} + \dfrac{8}{7}$ $\dfrac{1}{6} + \dfrac{1}{4}$

$\dfrac{9}{4} + \dfrac{3}{2}$ $\dfrac{1}{4} + \dfrac{5}{6}$ $\dfrac{1}{8} + \dfrac{4}{3}$ $\dfrac{3}{8} + \dfrac{1}{5}$ $\dfrac{1}{4} + \dfrac{7}{8}$

$\dfrac{9}{4} + \dfrac{1}{5}$ $\dfrac{5}{6} + \dfrac{5}{8}$ $\dfrac{1}{3} + \dfrac{7}{6}$ $\dfrac{4}{7} + \dfrac{5}{7}$ $\dfrac{4}{3} + \dfrac{1}{5}$

$\dfrac{3}{8} + \dfrac{3}{5}$ $\qquad$ $\dfrac{9}{2} + \dfrac{5}{7}$ $\qquad$ $\dfrac{3}{2} + \dfrac{3}{5}$ $\qquad$ $\dfrac{4}{3} + \dfrac{8}{5}$ $\qquad$ $\dfrac{5}{8} + \dfrac{8}{3}$

$\dfrac{4}{5} + \dfrac{1}{3}$ $\qquad$ $\dfrac{5}{9} + \dfrac{5}{4}$ $\qquad$ $\dfrac{3}{8} + \dfrac{4}{3}$ $\qquad$ $\dfrac{2}{7} + \dfrac{7}{4}$ $\qquad$ $\dfrac{3}{2} + \dfrac{1}{3}$

$\dfrac{3}{7} + \dfrac{6}{7}$ $\qquad$ $\dfrac{2}{9} + \dfrac{8}{9}$ $\qquad$ $\dfrac{7}{9} + \dfrac{3}{2}$ $\qquad$ $\dfrac{5}{7} + \dfrac{8}{9}$ $\qquad$ $\dfrac{2}{5} + \dfrac{4}{7}$

$\dfrac{9}{4} + \dfrac{9}{2}$ $\qquad$ $\dfrac{9}{5} + \dfrac{9}{4}$ $\qquad$ $\dfrac{9}{8} + \dfrac{2}{5}$ $\qquad$ $\dfrac{4}{9} + \dfrac{7}{9}$ $\qquad$ $\dfrac{7}{3} + \dfrac{8}{7}$

$\dfrac{2}{5} + \dfrac{7}{8}$ $\qquad$ $\dfrac{5}{9} + \dfrac{3}{8}$ $\qquad$ $\dfrac{9}{8} + \dfrac{3}{2}$ $\qquad$ $\dfrac{6}{7} + \dfrac{4}{9}$ $\qquad$ $\dfrac{3}{4} + \dfrac{8}{7}$

$\dfrac{9}{2} + \dfrac{9}{8}$ $\qquad$ $\dfrac{9}{2} + \dfrac{5}{3}$ $\qquad$ $\dfrac{5}{9} + \dfrac{6}{5}$ $\qquad$ $\dfrac{1}{5} + \dfrac{1}{4}$ $\qquad$ $\dfrac{8}{7} + \dfrac{8}{9}$

$\dfrac{5}{9} + \dfrac{7}{6}$ $\qquad$ $\dfrac{3}{7} + \dfrac{1}{2}$ $\qquad$ $\dfrac{1}{2} + \dfrac{2}{5}$ $\qquad$ $\dfrac{7}{6} + \dfrac{5}{7}$ $\qquad$ $\dfrac{7}{9} + \dfrac{7}{4}$

$\dfrac{1}{9} + \dfrac{3}{2}$ $\qquad$ $\dfrac{9}{5} + \dfrac{3}{4}$ $\qquad$ $\dfrac{1}{6} + \dfrac{6}{5}$ $\qquad$ $\dfrac{7}{8} + \dfrac{9}{2}$ $\qquad$ $\dfrac{7}{2} + \dfrac{2}{7}$

$\dfrac{5}{9} + \dfrac{9}{7}$ $\qquad$ $\dfrac{7}{4} + \dfrac{8}{5}$ $\qquad$ $\dfrac{1}{6} + \dfrac{7}{6}$ $\qquad$ $\dfrac{3}{4} + \dfrac{4}{5}$ $\qquad$ $\dfrac{7}{8} + \dfrac{3}{4}$

$\dfrac{8}{7} + \dfrac{9}{7}$ $\qquad$ $\dfrac{7}{6} + \dfrac{7}{6}$ $\qquad$ $\dfrac{7}{5} + \dfrac{3}{7}$ $\qquad$ $\dfrac{3}{8} + \dfrac{4}{9}$ $\qquad$ $\dfrac{3}{5} + \dfrac{5}{2}$

$\dfrac{7}{5} + \dfrac{4}{5}$ $\dfrac{2}{3} + \dfrac{1}{9}$ $\dfrac{7}{3} + \dfrac{5}{4}$ $\dfrac{7}{5} + \dfrac{4}{9}$ $\dfrac{2}{5} + \dfrac{2}{5}$

$\dfrac{8}{9} + \dfrac{2}{3}$ $\dfrac{1}{4} + \dfrac{8}{7}$ $\dfrac{2}{7} + \dfrac{3}{2}$ $\dfrac{3}{7} + \dfrac{6}{5}$ $\dfrac{6}{5} + \dfrac{2}{9}$

$\dfrac{2}{9} + \dfrac{8}{7}$ $\dfrac{1}{8} + \dfrac{9}{2}$ $\dfrac{7}{3} + \dfrac{3}{7}$ $\dfrac{9}{7} + \dfrac{5}{3}$ $\dfrac{5}{3} + \dfrac{1}{6}$

$\dfrac{5}{9} + \dfrac{8}{3}$ $\dfrac{6}{5} + \dfrac{7}{3}$ $\dfrac{7}{9} + \dfrac{7}{2}$ $\dfrac{7}{9} + \dfrac{9}{4}$ $\dfrac{2}{3} + \dfrac{5}{4}$

$\dfrac{3}{5} + \dfrac{9}{7}$ $\dfrac{1}{5} + \dfrac{1}{4}$ $\dfrac{6}{5} + \dfrac{9}{7}$ $\dfrac{1}{7} + \dfrac{4}{7}$ $\dfrac{1}{9} + \dfrac{5}{4}$

$\dfrac{7}{2} + \dfrac{5}{9}$　　　$\dfrac{9}{2} + \dfrac{4}{9}$　　　$\dfrac{1}{9} + \dfrac{8}{5}$　　　$\dfrac{3}{4} + \dfrac{1}{8}$　　　$\dfrac{4}{5} + \dfrac{7}{9}$

$\dfrac{1}{2} + \dfrac{1}{6}$　　　$\dfrac{7}{4} + \dfrac{1}{5}$　　　$\dfrac{1}{3} + \dfrac{9}{5}$　　　$\dfrac{9}{7} + \dfrac{6}{5}$　　　$\dfrac{4}{3} + \dfrac{5}{2}$

$\dfrac{5}{4} + \dfrac{9}{2}$　　　$\dfrac{5}{7} + \dfrac{3}{8}$　　　$\dfrac{6}{7} + \dfrac{1}{9}$　　　$\dfrac{9}{2} + \dfrac{5}{4}$　　　$\dfrac{5}{8} + \dfrac{3}{2}$

$\dfrac{9}{4} + \dfrac{1}{5}$　　　$\dfrac{7}{8} + \dfrac{2}{7}$　　　$\dfrac{7}{8} + \dfrac{9}{5}$　　　$\dfrac{3}{4} + \dfrac{3}{7}$　　　$\dfrac{6}{7} + \dfrac{4}{3}$

$\dfrac{2}{7} + \dfrac{9}{4}$　　　$\dfrac{6}{7} + \dfrac{9}{7}$　　　$\dfrac{4}{5} + \dfrac{9}{8}$　　　$\dfrac{2}{9} + \dfrac{1}{8}$　　　$\dfrac{2}{7} + \dfrac{1}{7}$

$\dfrac{8}{9} + \dfrac{5}{4}$ $\qquad$ $\dfrac{7}{8} + \dfrac{1}{7}$ $\qquad$ $\dfrac{7}{4} + \dfrac{7}{2}$ $\qquad$ $\dfrac{7}{5} + \dfrac{5}{8}$ $\qquad$ $\dfrac{5}{8} + \dfrac{4}{5}$

$\dfrac{7}{4} + \dfrac{2}{9}$ $\qquad$ $\dfrac{2}{5} + \dfrac{7}{4}$ $\qquad$ $\dfrac{6}{5} + \dfrac{7}{2}$ $\qquad$ $\dfrac{4}{7} + \dfrac{1}{9}$ $\qquad$ $\dfrac{1}{4} + \dfrac{9}{4}$

$\dfrac{4}{3} + \dfrac{3}{4}$ $\qquad$ $\dfrac{1}{3} + \dfrac{9}{2}$ $\qquad$ $\dfrac{3}{5} + \dfrac{3}{5}$ $\qquad$ $\dfrac{5}{6} + \dfrac{6}{7}$ $\qquad$ $\dfrac{8}{9} + \dfrac{1}{3}$

$\dfrac{2}{5} + \dfrac{2}{7}$ $\qquad$ $\dfrac{6}{7} + \dfrac{7}{3}$ $\qquad$ $\dfrac{5}{8} + \dfrac{5}{4}$ $\qquad$ $\dfrac{1}{4} + \dfrac{3}{2}$ $\qquad$ $\dfrac{7}{9} + \dfrac{1}{6}$

$\dfrac{7}{6} + \dfrac{1}{2}$ $\qquad$ $\dfrac{1}{6} + \dfrac{1}{5}$ $\qquad$ $\dfrac{1}{7} + \dfrac{1}{5}$ $\qquad$ $\dfrac{1}{6} + \dfrac{5}{8}$ $\qquad$ $\dfrac{4}{3} + \dfrac{6}{7}$

$\dfrac{1}{6} + \dfrac{1}{8}$ $\dfrac{1}{2} + \dfrac{7}{4}$ $\dfrac{8}{5} + \dfrac{9}{5}$ $\dfrac{1}{2} + \dfrac{1}{7}$ $\dfrac{2}{3} + \dfrac{7}{4}$

$\dfrac{1}{5} + \dfrac{1}{3}$ $\dfrac{4}{9} + \dfrac{8}{7}$ $\dfrac{7}{6} + \dfrac{3}{5}$ $\dfrac{1}{5} + \dfrac{5}{4}$ $\dfrac{5}{8} + \dfrac{5}{6}$

$\dfrac{7}{5} + \dfrac{8}{9}$ $\dfrac{1}{6} + \dfrac{1}{3}$ $\dfrac{1}{9} + \dfrac{7}{2}$ $\dfrac{4}{3} + \dfrac{3}{2}$ $\dfrac{8}{5} + \dfrac{3}{8}$

$\dfrac{2}{5} + \dfrac{1}{7}$ $\dfrac{1}{2} + \dfrac{7}{6}$ $\dfrac{3}{7} + \dfrac{9}{5}$ $\dfrac{8}{3} + \dfrac{1}{9}$ $\dfrac{1}{8} + \dfrac{8}{3}$

$\dfrac{3}{8} + \dfrac{4}{9}$ $\dfrac{6}{7} + \dfrac{6}{5}$ $\dfrac{9}{2} + \dfrac{4}{3}$ $\dfrac{7}{3} + \dfrac{9}{8}$ $\dfrac{9}{4} + \dfrac{8}{7}$

$\dfrac{4}{5} + \dfrac{7}{9}$ $\qquad$ $\dfrac{3}{2} + \dfrac{1}{6}$ $\qquad$ $\dfrac{1}{3} + \dfrac{1}{9}$ $\qquad$ $\dfrac{7}{6} + \dfrac{5}{7}$ $\qquad$ $\dfrac{4}{5} + \dfrac{5}{9}$

$\dfrac{2}{5} + \dfrac{1}{2}$ $\qquad$ $\dfrac{5}{9} + \dfrac{8}{7}$ $\qquad$ $\dfrac{7}{9} + \dfrac{5}{6}$ $\qquad$ $\dfrac{1}{6} + \dfrac{8}{3}$ $\qquad$ $\dfrac{3}{8} + \dfrac{7}{3}$

$\dfrac{2}{5} + \dfrac{2}{5}$ $\qquad$ $\dfrac{7}{8} + \dfrac{6}{7}$ $\qquad$ $\dfrac{9}{7} + \dfrac{5}{8}$ $\qquad$ $\dfrac{7}{9} + \dfrac{7}{6}$ $\qquad$ $\dfrac{3}{7} + \dfrac{2}{5}$

$\dfrac{8}{7} + \dfrac{8}{5}$ $\qquad$ $\dfrac{9}{4} + \dfrac{8}{7}$ $\qquad$ $\dfrac{5}{2} + \dfrac{1}{9}$ $\qquad$ $\dfrac{9}{8} + \dfrac{3}{2}$ $\qquad$ $\dfrac{7}{2} + \dfrac{7}{5}$

$\dfrac{1}{2} + \dfrac{7}{4}$ $\qquad$ $\dfrac{4}{3} + \dfrac{4}{7}$ $\qquad$ $\dfrac{1}{7} + \dfrac{2}{5}$ $\qquad$ $\dfrac{7}{4} + \dfrac{3}{2}$ $\qquad$ $\dfrac{4}{9} + \dfrac{8}{5}$

$$\frac{1}{6} + \frac{2}{9} \qquad \frac{1}{2} + \frac{8}{7} \qquad \frac{4}{5} + \frac{1}{4} \qquad \frac{2}{7} + \frac{9}{5} \qquad \frac{5}{8} + \frac{7}{2}$$

$$\frac{1}{6} + \frac{3}{7} \qquad \frac{2}{9} + \frac{8}{7} \qquad \frac{7}{2} + \frac{3}{7} \qquad \frac{5}{8} + \frac{3}{7} \qquad \frac{5}{2} + \frac{2}{7}$$

$$\frac{2}{7} + \frac{5}{3} \qquad \frac{6}{7} + \frac{2}{3} \qquad \frac{3}{5} + \frac{5}{2} \qquad \frac{8}{5} + \frac{5}{2} \qquad \frac{7}{5} + \frac{2}{7}$$

$$\frac{5}{2} + \frac{7}{5} \qquad \frac{1}{8} + \frac{9}{5} \qquad \frac{5}{6} + \frac{7}{8} \qquad \frac{3}{7} + \frac{4}{9} \qquad \frac{8}{5} + \frac{1}{5}$$

$$\frac{1}{5} + \frac{4}{9} \qquad \frac{9}{4} + \frac{1}{9} \qquad \frac{5}{3} + \frac{4}{7} \qquad \frac{7}{9} + \frac{8}{7} \qquad \frac{8}{9} + \frac{7}{2}$$

$\dfrac{7}{6} + \dfrac{8}{7}$ $\qquad$ $\dfrac{9}{2} + \dfrac{4}{5}$ $\qquad$ $\dfrac{1}{2} + \dfrac{7}{3}$ $\qquad$ $\dfrac{1}{9} + \dfrac{5}{6}$ $\qquad$ $\dfrac{4}{3} + \dfrac{1}{2}$

$\dfrac{2}{9} + \dfrac{7}{6}$ $\qquad$ $\dfrac{7}{4} + \dfrac{7}{6}$ $\qquad$ $\dfrac{7}{6} + \dfrac{7}{9}$ $\qquad$ $\dfrac{5}{4} + \dfrac{7}{3}$ $\qquad$ $\dfrac{2}{3} + \dfrac{5}{7}$

$\dfrac{1}{3} + \dfrac{3}{2}$ $\qquad$ $\dfrac{5}{7} + \dfrac{9}{4}$ $\qquad$ $\dfrac{5}{8} + \dfrac{3}{4}$ $\qquad$ $\dfrac{9}{7} + \dfrac{1}{3}$ $\qquad$ $\dfrac{4}{5} + \dfrac{9}{4}$

$\dfrac{5}{2} + \dfrac{2}{3}$ $\qquad$ $\dfrac{5}{2} + \dfrac{9}{7}$ $\qquad$ $\dfrac{1}{3} + \dfrac{9}{8}$ $\qquad$ $\dfrac{9}{4} + \dfrac{1}{4}$ $\qquad$ $\dfrac{3}{8} + \dfrac{3}{4}$

$\dfrac{5}{6} + \dfrac{7}{2}$ $\qquad$ $\dfrac{5}{9} + \dfrac{7}{6}$ $\qquad$ $\dfrac{1}{4} + \dfrac{5}{7}$ $\qquad$ $\dfrac{3}{7} + \dfrac{9}{8}$ $\qquad$ $\dfrac{1}{2} + \dfrac{6}{5}$

$\frac{4}{5} + \frac{9}{4}$
$\frac{5}{6} + \frac{5}{7}$
$\frac{3}{8} + \frac{7}{2}$
$\frac{3}{7} + \frac{3}{2}$
$\frac{5}{3} + \frac{7}{8}$

$\frac{1}{8} + \frac{6}{7}$
$\frac{4}{7} + \frac{8}{3}$
$\frac{7}{2} + \frac{3}{7}$
$\frac{7}{4} + \frac{5}{7}$
$\frac{1}{3} + \frac{1}{8}$

$\frac{1}{8} + \frac{1}{9}$
$\frac{3}{8} + \frac{2}{3}$
$\frac{3}{8} + \frac{7}{5}$
$\frac{4}{7} + \frac{5}{6}$
$\frac{5}{7} + \frac{1}{2}$

$\frac{7}{9} + \frac{5}{8}$
$\frac{4}{7} + \frac{8}{5}$
$\frac{1}{9} + \frac{9}{2}$
$\frac{2}{9} + \frac{1}{7}$
$\frac{8}{9} + \frac{7}{5}$

$\frac{7}{5} + \frac{7}{5}$
$\frac{1}{8} + \frac{8}{5}$
$\frac{5}{7} + \frac{7}{9}$
$\frac{7}{2} + \frac{1}{5}$
$\frac{3}{5} + \frac{2}{3}$

$\frac{7}{8} + \frac{9}{7}$ $\frac{7}{9} + \frac{3}{4}$ $\frac{9}{7} + \frac{5}{6}$ $\frac{3}{5} + \frac{9}{5}$ $\frac{5}{4} + \frac{4}{3}$

$\frac{5}{2} + \frac{7}{8}$ $\frac{3}{4} + \frac{5}{2}$ $\frac{9}{7} + \frac{2}{7}$ $\frac{5}{4} + \frac{4}{9}$ $\frac{7}{9} + \frac{1}{3}$

$\frac{1}{2} + \frac{2}{7}$ $\frac{3}{4} + \frac{6}{5}$ $\frac{2}{3} + \frac{1}{5}$ $\frac{1}{4} + \frac{1}{2}$ $\frac{2}{5} + \frac{7}{8}$

$\frac{7}{3} + \frac{2}{9}$ $\frac{9}{7} + \frac{8}{5}$ $\frac{4}{5} + \frac{1}{2}$ $\frac{3}{7} + \frac{1}{5}$ $\frac{3}{7} + \frac{3}{8}$

$\frac{9}{5} + \frac{5}{7}$ $\frac{1}{6} + \frac{5}{2}$ $\frac{8}{3} + \frac{1}{5}$ $\frac{3}{5} + \frac{3}{8}$ $\frac{5}{4} + \frac{5}{9}$

$\dfrac{9}{8} + \dfrac{4}{7}$ $\qquad$ $\dfrac{6}{5} + \dfrac{1}{9}$ $\qquad$ $\dfrac{5}{7} + \dfrac{6}{5}$ $\qquad$ $\dfrac{9}{8} + \dfrac{5}{3}$ $\qquad$ $\dfrac{3}{5} + \dfrac{2}{3}$

$\dfrac{3}{7} + \dfrac{5}{3}$ $\qquad$ $\dfrac{2}{7} + \dfrac{9}{8}$ $\qquad$ $\dfrac{5}{6} + \dfrac{8}{5}$ $\qquad$ $\dfrac{7}{2} + \dfrac{3}{7}$ $\qquad$ $\dfrac{5}{9} + \dfrac{7}{8}$

$\dfrac{3}{2} + \dfrac{6}{7}$ $\qquad$ $\dfrac{9}{5} + \dfrac{1}{9}$ $\qquad$ $\dfrac{9}{2} + \dfrac{8}{5}$ $\qquad$ $\dfrac{6}{5} + \dfrac{5}{9}$ $\qquad$ $\dfrac{1}{7} + \dfrac{3}{8}$

$\dfrac{3}{5} + \dfrac{5}{3}$ $\qquad$ $\dfrac{7}{3} + \dfrac{1}{2}$ $\qquad$ $\dfrac{3}{5} + \dfrac{2}{3}$ $\qquad$ $\dfrac{9}{5} + \dfrac{1}{4}$ $\qquad$ $\dfrac{1}{4} + \dfrac{3}{5}$

$\dfrac{9}{8} + \dfrac{3}{7}$ $\qquad$ $\dfrac{7}{3} + \dfrac{1}{6}$ $\qquad$ $\dfrac{1}{6} + \dfrac{7}{5}$ $\qquad$ $\dfrac{5}{8} + \dfrac{9}{7}$ $\qquad$ $\dfrac{8}{7} + \dfrac{5}{8}$

$\dfrac{7}{9} + \dfrac{1}{8}$ $\dfrac{1}{3} + \dfrac{4}{5}$ $\dfrac{3}{2} + \dfrac{4}{7}$ $\dfrac{4}{5} + \dfrac{7}{5}$ $\dfrac{5}{8} + \dfrac{4}{3}$

$\dfrac{2}{7} + \dfrac{9}{4}$ $\dfrac{7}{5} + \dfrac{5}{3}$ $\dfrac{9}{2} + \dfrac{7}{9}$ $\dfrac{5}{2} + \dfrac{1}{7}$ $\dfrac{1}{2} + \dfrac{2}{9}$

$\dfrac{3}{5} + \dfrac{8}{9}$ $\dfrac{1}{7} + \dfrac{3}{8}$ $\dfrac{1}{8} + \dfrac{4}{3}$ $\dfrac{9}{7} + \dfrac{3}{8}$ $\dfrac{7}{2} + \dfrac{8}{5}$

$\dfrac{1}{9} + \dfrac{2}{7}$ $\dfrac{2}{5} + \dfrac{9}{8}$ $\dfrac{9}{7} + \dfrac{3}{4}$ $\dfrac{1}{3} + \dfrac{3}{2}$ $\dfrac{1}{3} + \dfrac{1}{8}$

$\dfrac{8}{5} + \dfrac{4}{3}$ $\dfrac{7}{6} + \dfrac{1}{8}$ $\dfrac{3}{8} + \dfrac{2}{3}$ $\dfrac{9}{7} + \dfrac{1}{3}$ $\dfrac{3}{7} + \dfrac{8}{7}$

$\dfrac{9}{2} + \dfrac{9}{7}$ $\dfrac{3}{5} + \dfrac{9}{4}$ $\dfrac{5}{4} + \dfrac{1}{7}$ $\dfrac{6}{5} + \dfrac{7}{4}$ $\dfrac{4}{7} + \dfrac{5}{6}$

$\dfrac{7}{4} + \dfrac{5}{3}$ $\dfrac{5}{6} + \dfrac{3}{4}$ $\dfrac{5}{6} + \dfrac{4}{7}$ $\dfrac{1}{6} + \dfrac{1}{2}$ $\dfrac{7}{5} + \dfrac{7}{5}$

$\dfrac{2}{9} + \dfrac{1}{5}$ $\dfrac{1}{7} + \dfrac{2}{9}$ $\dfrac{6}{5} + \dfrac{1}{5}$ $\dfrac{1}{2} + \dfrac{1}{7}$ $\dfrac{1}{2} + \dfrac{5}{7}$

$\dfrac{9}{5} + \dfrac{3}{8}$ $\dfrac{7}{2} + \dfrac{7}{8}$ $\dfrac{7}{5} + \dfrac{6}{7}$ $\dfrac{8}{5} + \dfrac{9}{5}$ $\dfrac{7}{6} + \dfrac{2}{3}$

$\dfrac{1}{7} + \dfrac{3}{7}$ $\dfrac{1}{9} + \dfrac{7}{5}$ $\dfrac{7}{5} + \dfrac{5}{8}$ $\dfrac{1}{4} + \dfrac{9}{7}$ $\dfrac{1}{9} + \dfrac{3}{4}$

$\frac{3}{8} + \frac{1}{4}$ $\qquad$ $\frac{7}{8} + \frac{9}{5}$ $\qquad$ $\frac{1}{5} + \frac{6}{7}$ $\qquad$ $\frac{5}{3} + \frac{7}{2}$ $\qquad$ $\frac{5}{4} + \frac{1}{3}$

$\frac{7}{4} + \frac{1}{2}$ $\qquad$ $\frac{7}{5} + \frac{1}{4}$ $\qquad$ $\frac{6}{7} + \frac{8}{9}$ $\qquad$ $\frac{2}{5} + \frac{2}{7}$ $\qquad$ $\frac{5}{4} + \frac{1}{9}$

$\frac{3}{4} + \frac{1}{6}$ $\qquad$ $\frac{8}{3} + \frac{9}{7}$ $\qquad$ $\frac{1}{4} + \frac{6}{7}$ $\qquad$ $\frac{7}{6} + \frac{5}{8}$ $\qquad$ $\frac{5}{9} + \frac{8}{5}$

$\frac{3}{7} + \frac{1}{6}$ $\qquad$ $\frac{5}{8} + \frac{1}{9}$ $\qquad$ $\frac{3}{8} + \frac{2}{3}$ $\qquad$ $\frac{7}{5} + \frac{9}{8}$ $\qquad$ $\frac{6}{7} + \frac{3}{5}$

$\frac{7}{5} + \frac{9}{2}$ $\qquad$ $\frac{7}{6} + \frac{7}{4}$ $\qquad$ $\frac{4}{7} + \frac{9}{8}$ $\qquad$ $\frac{5}{4} + \frac{1}{6}$ $\qquad$ $\frac{6}{5} + \frac{7}{5}$

$\dfrac{8}{9} + \dfrac{9}{5}$
$\qquad$
$\dfrac{3}{5} + \dfrac{1}{6}$
$\qquad$
$\dfrac{5}{2} + \dfrac{9}{8}$
$\qquad$
$\dfrac{3}{2} + \dfrac{7}{8}$
$\qquad$
$\dfrac{3}{8} + \dfrac{8}{3}$

$\dfrac{8}{5} + \dfrac{8}{5}$
$\qquad$
$\dfrac{5}{4} + \dfrac{7}{6}$
$\qquad$
$\dfrac{6}{5} + \dfrac{4}{3}$
$\qquad$
$\dfrac{4}{9} + \dfrac{1}{4}$
$\qquad$
$\dfrac{3}{7} + \dfrac{1}{6}$

$\dfrac{5}{7} + \dfrac{5}{9}$
$\qquad$
$\dfrac{1}{4} + \dfrac{1}{5}$
$\qquad$
$\dfrac{1}{4} + \dfrac{6}{7}$
$\qquad$
$\dfrac{2}{5} + \dfrac{2}{9}$
$\qquad$
$\dfrac{1}{8} + \dfrac{5}{2}$

$\dfrac{7}{2} + \dfrac{2}{9}$
$\qquad$
$\dfrac{9}{2} + \dfrac{2}{7}$
$\qquad$
$\dfrac{8}{9} + \dfrac{9}{4}$
$\qquad$
$\dfrac{2}{7} + \dfrac{8}{5}$
$\qquad$
$\dfrac{3}{5} + \dfrac{6}{5}$

$\dfrac{4}{9} + \dfrac{3}{4}$
$\qquad$
$\dfrac{1}{5} + \dfrac{9}{2}$
$\qquad$
$\dfrac{3}{7} + \dfrac{4}{5}$
$\qquad$
$\dfrac{1}{4} + \dfrac{5}{3}$
$\qquad$
$\dfrac{9}{5} + \dfrac{5}{7}$

$\frac{4}{3} + \frac{4}{5}$ $\qquad$ $\frac{8}{7} + \frac{8}{7}$ $\qquad$ $\frac{8}{3} + \frac{3}{2}$ $\qquad$ $\frac{2}{9} + \frac{5}{2}$ $\qquad$ $\frac{5}{9} + \frac{4}{5}$

$\frac{4}{9} + \frac{4}{5}$ $\qquad$ $\frac{5}{8} + \frac{8}{9}$ $\qquad$ $\frac{3}{7} + \frac{1}{5}$ $\qquad$ $\frac{9}{5} + \frac{4}{3}$ $\qquad$ $\frac{7}{5} + \frac{9}{8}$

$\frac{5}{4} + \frac{1}{2}$ $\qquad$ $\frac{2}{7} + \frac{4}{5}$ $\qquad$ $\frac{2}{5} + \frac{5}{7}$ $\qquad$ $\frac{4}{5} + \frac{9}{5}$ $\qquad$ $\frac{5}{9} + \frac{2}{3}$

$\frac{9}{4} + \frac{7}{5}$ $\qquad$ $\frac{4}{5} + \frac{5}{9}$ $\qquad$ $\frac{3}{4} + \frac{3}{5}$ $\qquad$ $\frac{1}{9} + \frac{5}{6}$ $\qquad$ $\frac{9}{2} + \frac{6}{7}$

$\frac{8}{9} + \frac{1}{3}$ $\qquad$ $\frac{7}{4} + \frac{6}{7}$ $\qquad$ $\frac{3}{4} + \frac{2}{5}$ $\qquad$ $\frac{3}{7} + \frac{5}{3}$ $\qquad$ $\frac{7}{6} + \frac{9}{8}$

$$\frac{7}{2} + \frac{3}{7} \qquad \frac{4}{9} + \frac{4}{7} \qquad \frac{5}{9} + \frac{3}{4} \qquad \frac{5}{9} + \frac{5}{8} \qquad \frac{7}{4} + \frac{9}{5}$$

$$\frac{9}{2} + \frac{4}{5} \qquad \frac{1}{4} + \frac{5}{7} \qquad \frac{2}{3} + \frac{7}{5} \qquad \frac{9}{2} + \frac{9}{7} \qquad \frac{8}{9} + \frac{8}{9}$$

$$\frac{8}{3} + \frac{6}{7} \qquad \frac{7}{5} + \frac{4}{9} \qquad \frac{8}{3} + \frac{8}{7} \qquad \frac{1}{5} + \frac{1}{9} \qquad \frac{7}{3} + \frac{1}{2}$$

$$\frac{7}{8} + \frac{9}{5} \qquad \frac{8}{3} + \frac{9}{4} \qquad \frac{5}{6} + \frac{5}{3} \qquad \frac{1}{2} + \frac{1}{5} \qquad \frac{7}{6} + \frac{5}{4}$$

$$\frac{3}{2} + \frac{1}{3} \qquad \frac{1}{2} + \frac{3}{8} \qquad \frac{1}{2} + \frac{7}{6} \qquad \frac{5}{6} + \frac{6}{5} \qquad \frac{6}{5} + \frac{1}{8}$$

$\dfrac{5}{2} + \dfrac{1}{3}$ $\dfrac{4}{7} + \dfrac{5}{7}$ $\dfrac{4}{7} + \dfrac{5}{9}$ $\dfrac{7}{2} + \dfrac{7}{8}$ $\dfrac{5}{6} + \dfrac{5}{7}$

$\dfrac{7}{3} + \dfrac{3}{7}$ $\dfrac{8}{9} + \dfrac{8}{5}$ $\dfrac{2}{3} + \dfrac{5}{2}$ $\dfrac{9}{5} + \dfrac{9}{5}$ $\dfrac{7}{9} + \dfrac{1}{8}$

$\dfrac{4}{7} + \dfrac{6}{5}$ $\dfrac{6}{7} + \dfrac{2}{7}$ $\dfrac{4}{5} + \dfrac{3}{8}$ $\dfrac{1}{6} + \dfrac{8}{3}$ $\dfrac{7}{8} + \dfrac{2}{9}$

$\dfrac{1}{4} + \dfrac{2}{3}$ $\dfrac{8}{7} + \dfrac{9}{4}$ $\dfrac{2}{7} + \dfrac{5}{3}$ $\dfrac{2}{7} + \dfrac{5}{9}$ $\dfrac{1}{5} + \dfrac{1}{7}$

$\dfrac{3}{2} + \dfrac{1}{8}$ $\dfrac{4}{9} + \dfrac{1}{8}$ $\dfrac{3}{8} + \dfrac{9}{5}$ $\dfrac{4}{5} + \dfrac{6}{7}$ $\dfrac{1}{7} + \dfrac{7}{8}$

Part 2: Practice Subtracting Fractions

The strategy for subtracting two fractions is exactly the same as for adding two fractions except for subtracting, rather than adding, the two numerators after multiplying the numerator and denominator of each fraction by the factor needed to make the lowest common denominator.

EXAMPLES

$$\frac{4}{3} - \frac{3}{4}$$
$$= \frac{4 \cdot 4}{4 \cdot 3} - \frac{3 \cdot 3}{3 \cdot 4}$$
$$= \frac{16}{12} - \frac{9}{12}$$
$$= \frac{16 - 9}{12}$$
$$= \frac{7}{12}$$

$$\frac{5}{6} - \frac{1}{3}$$
$$= \frac{5}{6} - \frac{2 \cdot 1}{2 \cdot 3}$$
$$= \frac{5}{6} - \frac{2}{6}$$
$$= \frac{3}{6}$$
$$= \frac{1}{2}$$

$$\frac{5}{7} - \frac{2}{3} \qquad \frac{2}{3} - \frac{1}{8} \qquad \frac{5}{8} - \frac{1}{5} \qquad \frac{2}{5} - \frac{1}{6} \qquad \frac{9}{8} - \frac{5}{6}$$

$$\frac{8}{9} - \frac{6}{7} \qquad \frac{5}{3} - \frac{2}{7} \qquad \frac{3}{2} - \frac{4}{3} \qquad \frac{8}{5} - \frac{8}{9} \qquad \frac{3}{5} - \frac{1}{9}$$

$$\frac{8}{3} - \frac{1}{9} \qquad \frac{6}{5} - \frac{2}{3} \qquad \frac{5}{3} - \frac{3}{2} \qquad \frac{6}{7} - \frac{3}{8} \qquad \frac{2}{9} - \frac{1}{5}$$

$$\frac{9}{4} - \frac{8}{9} \qquad \frac{2}{5} - \frac{1}{5} \qquad \frac{7}{2} - \frac{7}{3} \qquad \frac{9}{4} - \frac{5}{9} \qquad \frac{2}{3} - \frac{4}{9}$$

$$\frac{8}{5} - \frac{2}{5} \qquad \frac{9}{5} - \frac{5}{6} \qquad \frac{9}{2} - \frac{2}{9} \qquad \frac{6}{5} - \frac{3}{5} \qquad \frac{6}{5} - \frac{7}{8}$$

$$\frac{5}{8} - \frac{1}{7} \qquad \frac{4}{5} - \frac{5}{8} \qquad \frac{7}{9} - \frac{5}{9} \qquad \frac{5}{2} - \frac{1}{8} \qquad \frac{7}{2} - \frac{1}{3}$$

$$\frac{4}{9} - \frac{2}{7} \qquad \frac{6}{5} - \frac{1}{8} \qquad \frac{3}{2} - \frac{3}{4} \qquad \frac{4}{3} - \frac{5}{8} \qquad \frac{7}{6} - \frac{3}{5}$$

$$\frac{3}{2} - \frac{2}{3} \qquad \frac{9}{4} - \frac{7}{6} \qquad \frac{3}{7} - \frac{1}{9} \qquad \frac{8}{7} - \frac{9}{8} \qquad \frac{4}{9} - \frac{3}{8}$$

$$\frac{5}{7} - \frac{4}{7} \qquad \frac{6}{7} - \frac{5}{6} \qquad \frac{6}{5} - \frac{1}{6} \qquad \frac{5}{2} - \frac{9}{4} \qquad \frac{3}{2} - \frac{1}{4}$$

$$\frac{9}{7} - \frac{8}{7} \qquad \frac{4}{3} - \frac{3}{7} \qquad \frac{7}{4} - \frac{1}{8} \qquad \frac{7}{3} - \frac{3}{5} \qquad \frac{7}{2} - \frac{7}{6}$$

Practice Adding, Subtracting, Multiplying, and Dividing Fractions Workbook

$$\frac{3}{7} - \frac{1}{3} \qquad \frac{4}{5} - \frac{3}{4} \qquad \frac{7}{8} - \frac{1}{5} \qquad \frac{8}{3} - \frac{4}{5} \qquad \frac{3}{8} - \frac{2}{7}$$

$$\frac{3}{2} - \frac{6}{5} \qquad \frac{8}{9} - \frac{7}{8} \qquad \frac{9}{8} - \frac{2}{5} \qquad \frac{7}{3} - \frac{6}{7} \qquad \frac{5}{4} - \frac{9}{8}$$

$$\frac{7}{4} - \frac{1}{6} \qquad \frac{8}{3} - \frac{1}{9} \qquad \frac{7}{3} - \frac{8}{5} \qquad \frac{5}{2} - \frac{6}{5} \qquad \frac{8}{5} - \frac{1}{4}$$

$$\frac{8}{3} - \frac{8}{5} \qquad \frac{5}{8} - \frac{3}{8} \qquad \frac{7}{5} - \frac{1}{2} \qquad \frac{8}{3} - \frac{7}{9} \qquad \frac{7}{2} - \frac{2}{5}$$

$$\frac{6}{5} - \frac{4}{5} \qquad \frac{9}{2} - \frac{8}{3} \qquad \frac{8}{9} - \frac{6}{7} \qquad \frac{3}{2} - \frac{7}{6} \qquad \frac{5}{3} - \frac{1}{3}$$

$$\frac{2}{3} - \frac{4}{7} \qquad \frac{7}{5} - \frac{3}{5} \qquad \frac{7}{3} - \frac{7}{9} \qquad \frac{8}{3} - \frac{7}{6} \qquad \frac{8}{7} - \frac{6}{7}$$

$$\frac{5}{3} - \frac{7}{5} \qquad \frac{6}{7} - \frac{2}{3} \qquad \frac{6}{7} - \frac{5}{8} \qquad \frac{7}{3} - \frac{1}{4} \qquad \frac{3}{4} - \frac{5}{9}$$

$$\frac{9}{4} - \frac{7}{4} \qquad \frac{7}{3} - \frac{1}{5} \qquad \frac{2}{3} - \frac{4}{9} \qquad \frac{7}{6} - \frac{5}{8} \qquad \frac{7}{4} - \frac{8}{7}$$

$$\frac{5}{2} - \frac{2}{9} \qquad \frac{7}{4} - \frac{4}{5} \qquad \frac{9}{8} - \frac{2}{7} \qquad \frac{8}{5} - \frac{4}{7} \qquad \frac{9}{4} - \frac{4}{9}$$

$$\frac{7}{6} - \frac{2}{9} \qquad \frac{7}{3} - \frac{5}{4} \qquad \frac{4}{3} - \frac{5}{4} \qquad \frac{5}{9} - \frac{2}{5} \qquad \frac{7}{2} - \frac{2}{9}$$

Practice Adding, Subtracting, Multiplying, and Dividing Fractions Workbook

$$\frac{9}{2} - \frac{4}{3} \qquad \frac{7}{3} - \frac{4}{7} \qquad \frac{5}{3} - \frac{4}{9} \qquad \frac{8}{7} - \frac{3}{4} \qquad \frac{7}{9} - \frac{4}{9}$$

$$\frac{8}{7} - \frac{5}{7} \qquad \frac{6}{5} - \frac{1}{2} \qquad \frac{5}{7} - \frac{4}{9} \qquad \frac{7}{4} - \frac{7}{8} \qquad \frac{5}{9} - \frac{3}{7}$$

$$\frac{4}{3} - \frac{7}{6} \qquad \frac{5}{4} - \frac{3}{8} \qquad \frac{9}{5} - \frac{5}{9} \qquad \frac{8}{7} - \frac{7}{9} \qquad \frac{9}{7} - \frac{6}{7}$$

$$\frac{1}{3} - \frac{1}{5} \qquad \frac{7}{6} - \frac{1}{3} \qquad \frac{7}{2} - \frac{1}{7} \qquad \frac{8}{7} - \frac{1}{2} \qquad \frac{7}{2} - \frac{7}{6}$$

$$\frac{5}{3} - \frac{7}{6} \qquad \frac{7}{2} - \frac{8}{9} \qquad \frac{3}{4} - \frac{2}{3} \qquad \frac{9}{5} - \frac{5}{8} \qquad \frac{9}{8} - \frac{4}{5}$$

$$\frac{2}{5} - \frac{1}{9} \qquad \frac{9}{2} - \frac{9}{5} \qquad \frac{5}{4} - \frac{5}{9} \qquad \frac{9}{2} - \frac{1}{9} \qquad \frac{8}{3} - \frac{3}{7}$$

$$\frac{5}{9} - \frac{2}{7} \qquad \frac{4}{9} - \frac{2}{7} \qquad \frac{8}{7} - \frac{4}{5} \qquad \frac{7}{5} - \frac{2}{3} \qquad \frac{1}{3} - \frac{1}{5}$$

$$\frac{9}{7} - \frac{3}{8} \qquad \frac{1}{2} - \frac{4}{9} \qquad \frac{2}{7} - \frac{2}{9} \qquad \frac{8}{9} - \frac{3}{8} \qquad \frac{4}{5} - \frac{2}{3}$$

$$\frac{6}{7} - \frac{2}{5} \qquad \frac{1}{3} - \frac{1}{7} \qquad \frac{9}{7} - \frac{1}{5} \qquad \frac{6}{7} - \frac{5}{8} \qquad \frac{7}{2} - \frac{6}{7}$$

$$\frac{3}{4} - \frac{5}{8} \qquad \frac{2}{7} - \frac{1}{8} \qquad \frac{5}{3} - \frac{6}{7} \qquad \frac{5}{4} - \frac{6}{7} \qquad \frac{5}{3} - \frac{5}{4}$$

$$\frac{9}{2} - \frac{5}{8} \qquad \frac{9}{8} - \frac{3}{5} \qquad \frac{7}{5} - \frac{2}{5} \qquad \frac{2}{9} - \frac{1}{5} \qquad \frac{5}{4} - \frac{5}{6}$$

$$\frac{7}{3} - \frac{5}{4} \qquad \frac{9}{8} - \frac{2}{3} \qquad \frac{8}{3} - \frac{2}{3} \qquad \frac{7}{2} - \frac{7}{5} \qquad \frac{7}{6} - \frac{4}{9}$$

$$\frac{7}{2} - \frac{2}{5} \qquad \frac{3}{2} - \frac{5}{9} \qquad \frac{9}{5} - \frac{2}{3} \qquad \frac{9}{5} - \frac{1}{4} \qquad \frac{1}{2} - \frac{1}{3}$$

$$\frac{9}{8} - \frac{4}{5} \qquad \frac{4}{3} - \frac{3}{8} \qquad \frac{3}{4} - \frac{3}{7} \qquad \frac{7}{5} - \frac{5}{4} \qquad \frac{5}{3} - \frac{3}{8}$$

$$\frac{6}{5} - \frac{7}{9} \qquad \frac{4}{9} - \frac{1}{3} \qquad \frac{8}{3} - \frac{1}{9} \qquad \frac{7}{2} - \frac{2}{9} \qquad \frac{9}{4} - \frac{1}{3}$$

$$\frac{3}{5} - \frac{2}{7} \qquad \frac{7}{2} - \frac{2}{3} \qquad \frac{5}{4} - \frac{1}{3} \qquad \frac{8}{9} - \frac{4}{7} \qquad \frac{4}{3} - \frac{1}{4}$$

$$\frac{5}{3} - \frac{4}{5} \qquad \frac{4}{9} - \frac{1}{4} \qquad \frac{9}{2} - \frac{6}{5} \qquad \frac{9}{4} - \frac{7}{8} \qquad \frac{9}{7} - \frac{3}{8}$$

$$\frac{8}{5} - \frac{7}{5} \qquad \frac{8}{7} - \frac{6}{7} \qquad \frac{5}{3} - \frac{9}{8} \qquad \frac{9}{4} - \frac{4}{5} \qquad \frac{9}{5} - \frac{4}{7}$$

$$\frac{9}{4} - \frac{8}{9} \qquad \frac{7}{9} - \frac{3}{5} \qquad \frac{5}{2} - \frac{6}{7} \qquad \frac{4}{3} - \frac{6}{5} \qquad \frac{4}{5} - \frac{5}{7}$$

$$\frac{9}{2} - \frac{7}{5} \qquad \frac{9}{5} - \frac{8}{5} \qquad \frac{4}{5} - \frac{3}{8} \qquad \frac{6}{5} - \frac{1}{9} \qquad \frac{7}{3} - \frac{9}{5}$$

$$\frac{5}{8} - \frac{3}{5} \qquad \frac{3}{2} - \frac{5}{8} \qquad \frac{6}{5} - \frac{6}{7} \qquad \frac{8}{5} - \frac{9}{8} \qquad \frac{7}{6} - \frac{3}{4}$$

$$\frac{9}{5} - \frac{2}{5} \qquad \frac{3}{4} - \frac{1}{8} \qquad \frac{5}{7} - \frac{1}{9} \qquad \frac{5}{6} - \frac{1}{6} \qquad \frac{8}{5} - \frac{2}{7}$$

$$\frac{5}{2} - \frac{1}{3} \qquad \frac{3}{2} - \frac{1}{9} \qquad \frac{2}{5} - \frac{2}{9} \qquad \frac{7}{3} - \frac{1}{2} \qquad \frac{4}{3} - \frac{3}{8}$$

$$\frac{4}{3} - \frac{2}{3} \qquad \frac{4}{9} - \frac{2}{5} \qquad \frac{9}{5} - \frac{8}{9} \qquad \frac{7}{5} - \frac{3}{8} \qquad \frac{3}{4} - \frac{1}{2}$$

$$\frac{7}{4} - \frac{1}{6} \qquad \frac{3}{2} - \frac{8}{7} \qquad \frac{9}{5} - \frac{1}{4} \qquad \frac{8}{3} - \frac{5}{7} \qquad \frac{5}{7} - \frac{2}{9}$$

$$\frac{4}{7} - \frac{3}{7} \qquad \frac{8}{5} - \frac{4}{7} \qquad \frac{2}{5} - \frac{1}{5} \qquad \frac{5}{2} - \frac{3}{4} \qquad \frac{6}{7} - \frac{2}{7}$$

$$\frac{3}{4} - \frac{2}{5} \qquad \frac{3}{4} - \frac{1}{9} \qquad \frac{2}{3} - \frac{1}{2} \qquad \frac{7}{6} - \frac{4}{5} \qquad \frac{1}{6} - \frac{1}{9}$$

$$\frac{3}{2} - \frac{5}{6} \qquad \frac{6}{7} - \frac{4}{9} \qquad \frac{7}{3} - \frac{1}{3} \qquad \frac{7}{8} - \frac{1}{8} \qquad \frac{9}{4} - \frac{6}{5}$$

$$\frac{9}{2} - \frac{3}{5} \qquad \frac{8}{5} - \frac{1}{3} \qquad \frac{8}{5} - \frac{1}{4} \qquad \frac{9}{8} - \frac{2}{3} \qquad \frac{7}{5} - \frac{3}{7}$$

$$\frac{6}{7} - \frac{2}{9} \qquad \frac{4}{7} - \frac{4}{9} \qquad \frac{5}{7} - \frac{3}{5} \qquad \frac{8}{5} - \frac{2}{7} \qquad \frac{5}{6} - \frac{1}{2}$$

$$\frac{5}{8} - \frac{3}{5} \qquad \frac{7}{4} - \frac{1}{9} \qquad \frac{7}{5} - \frac{1}{9} \qquad \frac{4}{3} - \frac{3}{7} \qquad \frac{7}{4} - \frac{8}{9}$$

$$\frac{5}{3} - \frac{8}{5} \qquad \frac{5}{4} - \frac{3}{7} \qquad \frac{8}{3} - \frac{7}{4} \qquad \frac{4}{5} - \frac{5}{9} \qquad \frac{7}{8} - \frac{1}{9}$$

$$\frac{4}{3} - \frac{9}{7} \qquad \frac{3}{4} - \frac{4}{9} \qquad \frac{9}{2} - \frac{7}{9} \qquad \frac{2}{9} - \frac{1}{8} \qquad \frac{9}{4} - \frac{3}{7}$$

$$\frac{8}{9} - \frac{6}{7} \qquad \frac{9}{5} - \frac{8}{9} \qquad \frac{6}{5} - \frac{4}{7} \qquad \frac{8}{9} - \frac{5}{9} \qquad \frac{2}{7} - \frac{1}{4}$$

$$\frac{1}{5} - \frac{1}{7} \qquad \frac{9}{4} - \frac{1}{3} \qquad \frac{3}{2} - \frac{6}{7} \qquad \frac{3}{2} - \frac{3}{4} \qquad \frac{5}{9} - \frac{2}{7}$$

$$\frac{7}{6} - \frac{8}{9} \qquad \frac{9}{8} - \frac{1}{5} \qquad \frac{8}{7} - \frac{4}{7} \qquad \frac{7}{6} - \frac{2}{5} \qquad \frac{5}{2} - \frac{1}{7}$$

$$\frac{2}{3} - \frac{3}{7} \qquad \frac{7}{3} - \frac{2}{9} \qquad \frac{5}{2} - \frac{9}{7} \qquad \frac{7}{5} - \frac{1}{9} \qquad \frac{7}{6} - \frac{9}{8}$$

$$\frac{9}{4} - \frac{5}{9} \qquad \frac{1}{2} - \frac{3}{8} \qquad \frac{3}{4} - \frac{3}{7} \qquad \frac{5}{6} - \frac{4}{7} \qquad \frac{9}{5} - \frac{7}{4}$$

$$\frac{3}{2} - \frac{5}{6} \qquad \frac{1}{3} - \frac{1}{4} \qquad \frac{5}{4} - \frac{1}{3} \qquad \frac{6}{7} - \frac{3}{8} \qquad \frac{7}{3} - \frac{6}{5}$$

$$\frac{5}{4} - \frac{7}{8} \qquad \frac{9}{7} - \frac{6}{7} \qquad \frac{8}{7} - \frac{2}{9} \qquad \frac{5}{4} - \frac{1}{2} \qquad \frac{9}{5} - \frac{1}{7}$$

$$\frac{7}{3} - \frac{1}{7} \qquad \frac{8}{7} - \frac{1}{9} \qquad \frac{9}{8} - \frac{5}{9} \qquad \frac{4}{9} - \frac{1}{6} \qquad \frac{4}{5} - \frac{2}{5}$$

$$\frac{7}{9} - \frac{1}{4} \qquad \frac{6}{5} - \frac{1}{6} \qquad \frac{9}{8} - \frac{5}{8} \qquad \frac{9}{8} - \frac{1}{2} \qquad \frac{9}{7} - \frac{5}{6}$$

$$\frac{8}{7} - \frac{1}{6} \qquad \frac{9}{5} - \frac{7}{5} \qquad \frac{9}{2} - \frac{5}{9} \qquad \frac{7}{2} - \frac{6}{5} \qquad \frac{3}{5} - \frac{1}{5}$$

$$\frac{5}{4} - \frac{1}{8} \qquad \frac{4}{3} - \frac{4}{7} \qquad \frac{6}{5} - \frac{2}{9} \qquad \frac{8}{3} - \frac{5}{9} \qquad \frac{5}{6} - \frac{3}{4}$$

$$\frac{2}{7} - \frac{1}{6} \qquad \frac{7}{2} - \frac{6}{5} \qquad \frac{7}{5} - \frac{8}{9} \qquad \frac{8}{3} - \frac{5}{6} \qquad \frac{4}{3} - \frac{1}{2}$$

$$\frac{2}{3} - \frac{3}{7} \qquad \frac{7}{3} - \frac{5}{3} \qquad \frac{7}{3} - \frac{5}{6} \qquad \frac{2}{3} - \frac{2}{9} \qquad \frac{9}{2} - \frac{4}{7}$$

$$\frac{7}{4} - \frac{7}{9} \qquad \frac{7}{2} - \frac{6}{5} \qquad \frac{9}{4} - \frac{5}{3} \qquad \frac{7}{3} - \frac{6}{7} \qquad \frac{2}{3} - \frac{2}{7}$$

$$\frac{9}{4} - \frac{6}{5} \qquad \frac{7}{4} - \frac{2}{3} \qquad \frac{5}{3} - \frac{5}{9} \qquad \frac{9}{7} - \frac{3}{5} \qquad \frac{8}{7} - \frac{5}{8}$$

$$\frac{3}{4} - \frac{2}{7} \qquad \frac{3}{5} - \frac{1}{3} \qquad \frac{3}{2} - \frac{1}{8} \qquad \frac{9}{8} - \frac{5}{9} \qquad \frac{7}{9} - \frac{1}{8}$$

$$\frac{5}{2} - \frac{5}{3} \qquad \frac{8}{7} - \frac{1}{8} \qquad \frac{1}{2} - \frac{2}{5} \qquad \frac{8}{9} - \frac{3}{7} \qquad \frac{6}{7} - \frac{7}{9}$$

$$\frac{8}{3} - \frac{6}{5} \qquad \frac{8}{9} - \frac{1}{8} \qquad \frac{4}{5} - \frac{3}{4} \qquad \frac{3}{5} - \frac{2}{5} \qquad \frac{5}{3} - \frac{2}{7}$$

$$\frac{7}{2} - \frac{1}{8} \qquad \frac{7}{2} - \frac{9}{5} \qquad \frac{7}{6} - \frac{1}{8} \qquad \frac{5}{4} - \frac{8}{7} \qquad \frac{5}{4} - \frac{1}{3}$$

$$\frac{3}{4} - \frac{2}{7} \qquad \frac{4}{3} - \frac{4}{9} \qquad \frac{5}{8} - \frac{4}{9} \qquad \frac{9}{7} - \frac{1}{7} \qquad \frac{8}{9} - \frac{2}{7}$$

$$\frac{6}{7} - \frac{5}{6} \qquad \frac{7}{4} - \frac{3}{7} \qquad \frac{1}{3} - \frac{2}{9} \qquad \frac{6}{5} - \frac{3}{8} \qquad \frac{7}{2} - \frac{2}{5}$$

$$\frac{9}{4} - \frac{8}{7} \qquad \frac{2}{3} - \frac{3}{7} \qquad \frac{8}{9} - \frac{1}{6} \qquad \frac{1}{6} - \frac{1}{8} \qquad \frac{3}{4} - \frac{1}{6}$$

$$\frac{7}{2} - \frac{8}{5} \qquad \frac{5}{7} - \frac{5}{9} \qquad \frac{9}{2} - \frac{3}{4} \qquad \frac{7}{6} - \frac{3}{7} \qquad \frac{7}{6} - \frac{1}{9}$$

$$\frac{7}{3} - \frac{8}{7} \qquad \frac{1}{8} - \frac{1}{9} \qquad \frac{1}{7} - \frac{1}{9} \qquad \frac{9}{5} - \frac{7}{4} \qquad \frac{3}{2} - \frac{2}{5}$$

$$\frac{9}{2} - \frac{7}{3} \qquad \frac{4}{5} - \frac{2}{5} \qquad \frac{3}{7} - \frac{2}{9} \qquad \frac{5}{6} - \frac{7}{9} \qquad \frac{3}{4} - \frac{5}{8}$$

$$\frac{7}{5} - \frac{8}{9} \qquad \frac{9}{7} - \frac{1}{2} \qquad \frac{4}{5} - \frac{1}{7} \qquad \frac{5}{3} - \frac{1}{8} \qquad \frac{5}{2} - \frac{5}{8}$$

$$\frac{9}{5} - \frac{3}{4} \qquad \frac{7}{3} - \frac{5}{8} \qquad \frac{7}{5} - \frac{1}{6} \qquad \frac{6}{7} - \frac{4}{7} \qquad \frac{9}{7} - \frac{7}{8}$$

$\dfrac{9}{5} - \dfrac{5}{6}$ $\dfrac{2}{7} - \dfrac{1}{6}$ $\dfrac{7}{5} - \dfrac{1}{4}$ $\dfrac{8}{5} - \dfrac{4}{7}$ $\dfrac{3}{2} - \dfrac{5}{6}$

$\dfrac{5}{2} - \dfrac{1}{2}$ $\dfrac{4}{5} - \dfrac{2}{5}$ $\dfrac{7}{3} - \dfrac{1}{8}$ $\dfrac{5}{8} - \dfrac{1}{6}$ $\dfrac{4}{3} - \dfrac{1}{8}$

$\dfrac{7}{2} - \dfrac{3}{4}$ $\dfrac{1}{2} - \dfrac{1}{7}$ $\dfrac{7}{4} - \dfrac{9}{7}$ $\dfrac{9}{2} - \dfrac{7}{2}$ $\dfrac{8}{9} - \dfrac{7}{9}$

$\dfrac{7}{9} - \dfrac{1}{5}$ $\dfrac{3}{2} - \dfrac{1}{3}$ $\dfrac{3}{8} - \dfrac{1}{9}$ $\dfrac{8}{3} - \dfrac{5}{9}$ $\dfrac{7}{3} - \dfrac{7}{9}$

$\dfrac{7}{2} - \dfrac{4}{7}$ $\dfrac{7}{2} - \dfrac{8}{9}$ $\dfrac{7}{3} - \dfrac{5}{3}$ $\dfrac{7}{5} - \dfrac{1}{5}$ $\dfrac{8}{5} - \dfrac{2}{3}$

$$\frac{7}{2} - \frac{8}{3} \qquad \frac{7}{5} - \frac{3}{7} \qquad \frac{8}{5} - \frac{1}{6} \qquad \frac{6}{7} - \frac{1}{2} \qquad \frac{9}{8} - \frac{2}{5}$$

$$\frac{7}{5} - \frac{1}{8} \qquad \frac{6}{7} - \frac{4}{9} \qquad \frac{7}{5} - \frac{5}{6} \qquad \frac{2}{3} - \frac{1}{7} \qquad \frac{3}{2} - \frac{4}{9}$$

$$\frac{7}{6} - \frac{1}{3} \qquad \frac{7}{6} - \frac{4}{5} \qquad \frac{4}{5} - \frac{2}{7} \qquad \frac{3}{7} - \frac{2}{7} \qquad \frac{7}{5} - \frac{6}{5}$$

$$\frac{7}{9} - \frac{2}{3} \qquad \frac{7}{3} - \frac{2}{7} \qquad \frac{3}{7} - \frac{3}{8} \qquad \frac{9}{4} - \frac{3}{5} \qquad \frac{5}{3} - \frac{5}{7}$$

$$\frac{8}{3} - \frac{4}{9} \qquad \frac{9}{2} - \frac{5}{2} \qquad \frac{7}{6} - \frac{3}{7} \qquad \frac{7}{6} - \frac{5}{8} \qquad \frac{7}{2} - \frac{4}{7}$$

$$\frac{7}{6} - \frac{7}{9} \qquad \frac{5}{2} - \frac{5}{3} \qquad \frac{6}{7} - \frac{7}{9} \qquad \frac{4}{5} - \frac{3}{8} \qquad \frac{9}{4} - \frac{7}{5}$$

$$\frac{9}{2} - \frac{5}{7} \qquad \frac{7}{8} - \frac{1}{5} \qquad \frac{9}{7} - \frac{4}{5} \qquad \frac{3}{8} - \frac{2}{9} \qquad \frac{5}{2} - \frac{8}{7}$$

$$\frac{6}{7} - \frac{4}{7} \qquad \frac{3}{2} - \frac{6}{5} \qquad \frac{5}{2} - \frac{1}{4} \qquad \frac{5}{3} - \frac{2}{7} \qquad \frac{3}{2} - \frac{3}{4}$$

$$\frac{9}{7} - \frac{6}{7} \qquad \frac{9}{5} - \frac{6}{7} \qquad \frac{7}{2} - \frac{8}{9} \qquad \frac{7}{3} - \frac{1}{9} \qquad \frac{6}{5} - \frac{7}{8}$$

$$\frac{8}{9} - \frac{6}{7} \qquad \frac{6}{7} - \frac{7}{9} \qquad \frac{7}{6} - \frac{9}{8} \qquad \frac{9}{5} - \frac{9}{7} \qquad \frac{3}{2} - \frac{1}{3}$$

$$\frac{9}{8} - \frac{5}{6} \qquad \frac{4}{5} - \frac{2}{7} \qquad \frac{5}{8} - \frac{3}{8} \qquad \frac{6}{5} - \frac{4}{5} \qquad \frac{3}{2} - \frac{6}{7}$$

$$\frac{7}{8} - \frac{5}{8} \qquad \frac{2}{5} - \frac{2}{7} \qquad \frac{4}{5} - \frac{2}{9} \qquad \frac{4}{7} - \frac{2}{5} \qquad \frac{8}{5} - \frac{8}{7}$$

$$\frac{7}{5} - \frac{7}{8} \qquad \frac{7}{8} - \frac{1}{7} \qquad \frac{3}{4} - \frac{1}{3} \qquad \frac{7}{4} - \frac{5}{7} \qquad \frac{4}{3} - \frac{5}{7}$$

$$\frac{7}{2} - \frac{9}{4} \qquad \frac{9}{2} - \frac{1}{2} \qquad \frac{4}{3} - \frac{2}{3} \qquad \frac{5}{8} - \frac{1}{9} \qquad \frac{6}{5} - \frac{5}{8}$$

$$\frac{6}{5} - \frac{7}{6} \qquad \frac{7}{4} - \frac{4}{9} \qquad \frac{5}{4} - \frac{9}{8} \qquad \frac{4}{7} - \frac{1}{6} \qquad \frac{8}{3} - \frac{7}{5}$$

$$\frac{7}{2} - \frac{2}{7} \qquad \frac{9}{5} - \frac{9}{7} \qquad \frac{5}{8} - \frac{3}{7} \qquad \frac{2}{5} - \frac{2}{9} \qquad \frac{3}{5} - \frac{2}{7}$$

$$\frac{4}{3} - \frac{1}{2} \qquad \frac{9}{4} - \frac{4}{7} \qquad \frac{9}{8} - \frac{7}{9} \qquad \frac{5}{3} - \frac{6}{7} \qquad \frac{7}{5} - \frac{2}{9}$$

$$\frac{8}{3} - \frac{2}{7} \qquad \frac{3}{2} - \frac{1}{5} \qquad \frac{3}{8} - \frac{1}{9} \qquad \frac{8}{5} - \frac{3}{2} \qquad \frac{3}{2} - \frac{1}{8}$$

$$\frac{5}{3} - \frac{3}{5} \qquad \frac{5}{4} - \frac{5}{6} \qquad \frac{5}{4} - \frac{1}{7} \qquad \frac{8}{7} - \frac{2}{3} \qquad \frac{8}{5} - \frac{3}{2}$$

$$\frac{3}{2} - \frac{6}{7} \qquad \frac{7}{3} - \frac{1}{2} \qquad \frac{8}{3} - \frac{1}{7} \qquad \frac{2}{9} - \frac{1}{9} \qquad \frac{8}{5} - \frac{5}{7}$$

$$\frac{6}{5} - \frac{1}{6} \qquad \frac{7}{4} - \frac{4}{5} \qquad \frac{5}{2} - \frac{1}{7} \qquad \frac{1}{2} - \frac{4}{9} \qquad \frac{9}{4} - \frac{5}{9}$$

$$\frac{9}{4} - \frac{3}{2} \qquad \frac{4}{9} - \frac{1}{5} \qquad \frac{6}{5} - \frac{3}{5} \qquad \frac{5}{8} - \frac{1}{5} \qquad \frac{7}{4} - \frac{8}{7}$$

$$\frac{7}{2} - \frac{7}{5} \qquad \frac{7}{8} - \frac{1}{4} \qquad \frac{6}{5} - \frac{2}{7} \qquad \frac{5}{4} - \frac{5}{9} \qquad \frac{9}{5} - \frac{3}{7}$$

$$\frac{3}{2} - \frac{5}{7} \qquad \frac{7}{3} - \frac{6}{7} \qquad \frac{5}{7} - \frac{3}{8} \qquad \frac{4}{7} - \frac{5}{9} \qquad \frac{7}{8} - \frac{4}{9}$$

$$\frac{5}{3} - \frac{3}{7} \qquad \frac{8}{3} - \frac{5}{8} \qquad \frac{5}{3} - \frac{1}{7} \qquad \frac{7}{6} - \frac{5}{9} \qquad \frac{5}{6} - \frac{1}{2}$$

$$\frac{7}{3} - \frac{2}{5} \qquad \frac{9}{4} - \frac{5}{7} \qquad \frac{9}{4} - \frac{6}{5} \qquad \frac{6}{7} - \frac{1}{5} \qquad \frac{8}{5} - \frac{4}{5}$$

$$\frac{5}{4} - \frac{1}{6} \qquad \frac{7}{9} - \frac{5}{9} \qquad \frac{8}{9} - \frac{7}{9} \qquad \frac{8}{7} - \frac{2}{7} \qquad \frac{5}{3} - \frac{2}{5}$$

$$\frac{3}{5} - \frac{4}{9} \qquad \frac{4}{5} - \frac{1}{3} \qquad \frac{8}{5} - \frac{3}{4} \qquad \frac{9}{7} - \frac{6}{5} \qquad \frac{6}{5} - \frac{3}{8}$$

$$\frac{7}{4} - \frac{8}{9} \qquad \frac{9}{5} - \frac{5}{4} \qquad \frac{7}{8} - \frac{4}{7} \qquad \frac{3}{2} - \frac{4}{9} \qquad \frac{4}{5} - \frac{1}{9}$$

$$\frac{8}{7} - \frac{2}{7} \qquad \frac{5}{3} - \frac{7}{8} \qquad \frac{9}{4} - \frac{2}{3} \qquad \frac{5}{3} - \frac{1}{4} \qquad \frac{7}{3} - \frac{3}{7}$$

$$\frac{8}{9} - \frac{6}{7} \qquad \frac{7}{5} - \frac{4}{3} \qquad \frac{7}{6} - \frac{4}{9} \qquad \frac{8}{3} - \frac{1}{4} \qquad \frac{3}{4} - \frac{3}{7}$$

$$\frac{3}{5} - \frac{1}{8} \qquad \frac{7}{5} - \frac{3}{8} \qquad \frac{4}{7} - \frac{4}{9} \qquad \frac{9}{5} - \frac{6}{7} \qquad \frac{3}{4} - \frac{2}{5}$$

$$\frac{9}{7} - \frac{1}{9} \qquad \frac{5}{7} - \frac{1}{4} \qquad \frac{9}{2} - \frac{4}{3} \qquad \frac{9}{5} - \frac{6}{5} \qquad \frac{5}{7} - \frac{2}{5}$$

$$\frac{7}{6} - \frac{8}{9} \qquad \frac{4}{3} - \frac{1}{8} \qquad \frac{5}{3} - \frac{8}{7} \qquad \frac{7}{5} - \frac{2}{9} \qquad \frac{8}{3} - \frac{4}{5}$$

$$\frac{4}{3} - \frac{1}{5} \qquad \frac{9}{4} - \frac{8}{7} \qquad \frac{7}{6} - \frac{4}{7} \qquad \frac{6}{7} - \frac{3}{5} \qquad \frac{8}{9} - \frac{5}{9}$$

$\dfrac{4}{3} - \dfrac{1}{2}$ $\qquad$ $\dfrac{9}{2} - \dfrac{4}{5}$ $\qquad$ $\dfrac{9}{5} - \dfrac{5}{7}$ $\qquad$ $\dfrac{4}{3} - \dfrac{2}{5}$ $\qquad$ $\dfrac{9}{5} - \dfrac{8}{9}$

$\dfrac{9}{8} - \dfrac{5}{6}$ $\qquad$ $\dfrac{3}{8} - \dfrac{1}{9}$ $\qquad$ $\dfrac{3}{5} - \dfrac{2}{5}$ $\qquad$ $\dfrac{4}{3} - \dfrac{2}{3}$ $\qquad$ $\dfrac{5}{8} - \dfrac{5}{9}$

$\dfrac{7}{4} - \dfrac{4}{9}$ $\qquad$ $\dfrac{9}{5} - \dfrac{5}{8}$ $\qquad$ $\dfrac{5}{4} - \dfrac{3}{7}$ $\qquad$ $\dfrac{8}{3} - \dfrac{2}{3}$ $\qquad$ $\dfrac{4}{3} - \dfrac{4}{5}$

$\dfrac{6}{5} - \dfrac{1}{2}$ $\qquad$ $\dfrac{2}{7} - \dfrac{1}{5}$ $\qquad$ $\dfrac{7}{6} - \dfrac{6}{7}$ $\qquad$ $\dfrac{7}{3} - \dfrac{2}{3}$ $\qquad$ $\dfrac{5}{4} - \dfrac{4}{7}$

$\dfrac{7}{9} - \dfrac{4}{7}$ $\qquad$ $\dfrac{3}{5} - \dfrac{3}{7}$ $\qquad$ $\dfrac{7}{3} - \dfrac{7}{9}$ $\qquad$ $\dfrac{5}{7} - \dfrac{4}{7}$ $\qquad$ $\dfrac{7}{2} - \dfrac{9}{4}$

Part 3: Practice Multiplying Fractions

Multiplying two fractions is actually simpler than adding or subtracting two fractions because it is not necessary to find a common denominator in order to multiply fractions. In order to multiply two fractions, simply multiply the numerators together to make the new numerator and multiply the denominators together to make the new denominator. The resulting fraction may need to be reduced.

EXAMPLES

$$\frac{4}{3} \times \frac{1}{2}$$
$$= \frac{4 \cdot 1}{3 \cdot 2}$$
$$= \frac{4}{6}$$
$$= \frac{2}{3}$$

$$\frac{2}{3} \times \frac{6}{5}$$
$$= \frac{2 \cdot 6}{3 \cdot 5}$$
$$= \frac{12}{15}$$
$$= \frac{4}{5}$$

It is sometimes more efficient to reduce the fraction before multiplying the numbers together in the numerator and denominator. In the example above, the 2 times 6 divided by 3 times 5 can be reduced to 2 times 2 divided by 1 times 5, giving the reduced answer of 4/5 more readily. The point is that it is simpler to cancel the greatest common factor before multiplying the numbers together in the numerator and denominator.

$\frac{6}{7} \times \frac{4}{5}$ $\frac{3}{4} \times \frac{7}{9}$ $\frac{1}{8} \times \frac{7}{4}$ $\frac{4}{3} \times \frac{4}{7}$ $\frac{2}{9} \times \frac{6}{5}$

$\frac{1}{4} \times \frac{3}{7}$ $\frac{1}{6} \times \frac{9}{8}$ $\frac{7}{5} \times \frac{7}{5}$ $\frac{4}{5} \times \frac{9}{7}$ $\frac{9}{5} \times \frac{1}{4}$

$\frac{1}{7} \times \frac{7}{4}$ $\frac{9}{5} \times \frac{1}{2}$ $\frac{7}{8} \times \frac{7}{3}$ $\frac{1}{7} \times \frac{1}{2}$ $\frac{3}{4} \times \frac{7}{4}$

$\frac{8}{3} \times \frac{8}{9}$ $\frac{5}{2} \times \frac{3}{8}$ $\frac{1}{4} \times \frac{7}{3}$ $\frac{2}{9} \times \frac{2}{5}$ $\frac{5}{2} \times \frac{8}{3}$

$\frac{7}{8} \times \frac{1}{8}$ $\frac{3}{5} \times \frac{1}{9}$ $\frac{5}{2} \times \frac{1}{5}$ $\frac{2}{9} \times \frac{8}{3}$ $\frac{3}{2} \times \frac{8}{9}$

$\dfrac{4}{3} \times \dfrac{4}{9}$ $\qquad$ $\dfrac{4}{7} \times \dfrac{7}{5}$ $\qquad$ $\dfrac{1}{6} \times \dfrac{1}{8}$ $\qquad$ $\dfrac{1}{6} \times \dfrac{9}{2}$ $\qquad$ $\dfrac{3}{2} \times \dfrac{3}{2}$

$\dfrac{9}{7} \times \dfrac{9}{5}$ $\qquad$ $\dfrac{5}{4} \times \dfrac{5}{4}$ $\qquad$ $\dfrac{7}{5} \times \dfrac{2}{9}$ $\qquad$ $\dfrac{5}{6} \times \dfrac{2}{3}$ $\qquad$ $\dfrac{6}{7} \times \dfrac{8}{5}$

$\dfrac{9}{4} \times \dfrac{9}{5}$ $\qquad$ $\dfrac{3}{8} \times \dfrac{9}{7}$ $\qquad$ $\dfrac{2}{9} \times \dfrac{1}{8}$ $\qquad$ $\dfrac{1}{9} \times \dfrac{8}{7}$ $\qquad$ $\dfrac{5}{4} \times \dfrac{7}{6}$

$\dfrac{2}{3} \times \dfrac{8}{7}$ $\qquad$ $\dfrac{2}{9} \times \dfrac{2}{7}$ $\qquad$ $\dfrac{8}{3} \times \dfrac{7}{8}$ $\qquad$ $\dfrac{2}{9} \times \dfrac{1}{8}$ $\qquad$ $\dfrac{1}{4} \times \dfrac{9}{5}$

$\dfrac{2}{3} \times \dfrac{1}{7}$ $\qquad$ $\dfrac{6}{5} \times \dfrac{7}{4}$ $\qquad$ $\dfrac{5}{9} \times \dfrac{3}{4}$ $\qquad$ $\dfrac{1}{5} \times \dfrac{1}{9}$ $\qquad$ $\dfrac{9}{8} \times \dfrac{5}{8}$

$\dfrac{2}{5} \times \dfrac{3}{8}$ $\dfrac{4}{3} \times \dfrac{8}{5}$ $\dfrac{3}{2} \times \dfrac{7}{9}$ $\dfrac{7}{4} \times \dfrac{4}{5}$ $\dfrac{5}{7} \times \dfrac{6}{5}$

$\dfrac{8}{3} \times \dfrac{7}{3}$ $\dfrac{7}{2} \times \dfrac{5}{3}$ $\dfrac{5}{9} \times \dfrac{9}{4}$ $\dfrac{3}{2} \times \dfrac{9}{7}$ $\dfrac{4}{5} \times \dfrac{9}{7}$

$\dfrac{4}{7} \times \dfrac{3}{7}$ $\dfrac{1}{7} \times \dfrac{3}{5}$ $\dfrac{1}{9} \times \dfrac{1}{5}$ $\dfrac{7}{2} \times \dfrac{2}{5}$ $\dfrac{8}{9} \times \dfrac{5}{2}$

$\dfrac{7}{5} \times \dfrac{1}{4}$ $\dfrac{5}{6} \times \dfrac{8}{9}$ $\dfrac{4}{5} \times \dfrac{2}{5}$ $\dfrac{3}{5} \times \dfrac{2}{7}$ $\dfrac{5}{8} \times \dfrac{7}{3}$

$\dfrac{6}{7} \times \dfrac{8}{9}$ $\dfrac{9}{5} \times \dfrac{7}{3}$ $\dfrac{4}{3} \times \dfrac{2}{9}$ $\dfrac{1}{6} \times \dfrac{8}{9}$ $\dfrac{4}{9} \times \dfrac{2}{7}$

$\dfrac{7}{8} \times \dfrac{7}{4}$ $\qquad$ $\dfrac{9}{7} \times \dfrac{1}{7}$ $\qquad$ $\dfrac{3}{2} \times \dfrac{3}{8}$ $\qquad$ $\dfrac{7}{6} \times \dfrac{2}{5}$ $\qquad$ $\dfrac{3}{2} \times \dfrac{2}{9}$

$\dfrac{7}{8} \times \dfrac{5}{9}$ $\qquad$ $\dfrac{9}{7} \times \dfrac{8}{7}$ $\qquad$ $\dfrac{7}{5} \times \dfrac{9}{4}$ $\qquad$ $\dfrac{3}{4} \times \dfrac{1}{3}$ $\qquad$ $\dfrac{7}{2} \times \dfrac{1}{6}$

$\dfrac{3}{2} \times \dfrac{7}{9}$ $\qquad$ $\dfrac{2}{3} \times \dfrac{5}{8}$ $\qquad$ $\dfrac{8}{9} \times \dfrac{1}{7}$ $\qquad$ $\dfrac{5}{6} \times \dfrac{5}{3}$ $\qquad$ $\dfrac{9}{7} \times \dfrac{9}{8}$

$\dfrac{5}{7} \times \dfrac{7}{2}$ $\qquad$ $\dfrac{5}{8} \times \dfrac{2}{5}$ $\qquad$ $\dfrac{7}{4} \times \dfrac{5}{7}$ $\qquad$ $\dfrac{9}{2} \times \dfrac{9}{4}$ $\qquad$ $\dfrac{9}{5} \times \dfrac{7}{5}$

$\dfrac{3}{4} \times \dfrac{1}{3}$ $\qquad$ $\dfrac{7}{6} \times \dfrac{5}{2}$ $\qquad$ $\dfrac{7}{4} \times \dfrac{7}{4}$ $\qquad$ $\dfrac{4}{3} \times \dfrac{5}{7}$ $\qquad$ $\dfrac{3}{8} \times \dfrac{5}{8}$

$\dfrac{6}{7} \times \dfrac{7}{8}$ $\dfrac{3}{7} \times \dfrac{5}{4}$ $\dfrac{7}{9} \times \dfrac{5}{8}$ $\dfrac{1}{4} \times \dfrac{9}{7}$ $\dfrac{1}{3} \times \dfrac{7}{9}$

$\dfrac{9}{2} \times \dfrac{5}{9}$ $\dfrac{2}{5} \times \dfrac{6}{5}$ $\dfrac{9}{7} \times \dfrac{5}{8}$ $\dfrac{1}{7} \times \dfrac{2}{3}$ $\dfrac{5}{4} \times \dfrac{5}{9}$

$\dfrac{1}{3} \times \dfrac{2}{3}$ $\dfrac{4}{5} \times \dfrac{1}{6}$ $\dfrac{5}{9} \times \dfrac{9}{8}$ $\dfrac{5}{6} \times \dfrac{5}{6}$ $\dfrac{3}{4} \times \dfrac{1}{6}$

$\dfrac{7}{3} \times \dfrac{3}{4}$ $\dfrac{2}{5} \times \dfrac{5}{3}$ $\dfrac{1}{8} \times \dfrac{8}{5}$ $\dfrac{1}{4} \times \dfrac{8}{9}$ $\dfrac{7}{8} \times \dfrac{3}{8}$

$\dfrac{5}{9} \times \dfrac{9}{7}$ $\dfrac{5}{6} \times \dfrac{5}{6}$ $\dfrac{5}{4} \times \dfrac{3}{8}$ $\dfrac{9}{5} \times \dfrac{5}{4}$ $\dfrac{5}{8} \times \dfrac{1}{7}$

$\dfrac{1}{4} \times \dfrac{1}{8}$ $\dfrac{1}{8} \times \dfrac{4}{9}$ $\dfrac{5}{8} \times \dfrac{9}{8}$ $\dfrac{1}{6} \times \dfrac{5}{6}$ $\dfrac{9}{7} \times \dfrac{3}{2}$

$\dfrac{7}{8} \times \dfrac{5}{6}$ $\dfrac{1}{7} \times \dfrac{9}{7}$ $\dfrac{1}{5} \times \dfrac{5}{2}$ $\dfrac{5}{8} \times \dfrac{5}{2}$ $\dfrac{8}{7} \times \dfrac{2}{5}$

$\dfrac{8}{9} \times \dfrac{9}{7}$ $\dfrac{1}{3} \times \dfrac{8}{7}$ $\dfrac{1}{2} \times \dfrac{3}{2}$ $\dfrac{5}{8} \times \dfrac{9}{8}$ $\dfrac{3}{5} \times \dfrac{8}{7}$

$\dfrac{3}{8} \times \dfrac{5}{8}$ $\dfrac{1}{7} \times \dfrac{8}{7}$ $\dfrac{5}{2} \times \dfrac{5}{4}$ $\dfrac{3}{5} \times \dfrac{8}{7}$ $\dfrac{4}{5} \times \dfrac{2}{7}$

$\dfrac{4}{3} \times \dfrac{8}{9}$ $\dfrac{1}{3} \times \dfrac{5}{9}$ $\dfrac{7}{3} \times \dfrac{9}{8}$ $\dfrac{4}{5} \times \dfrac{8}{7}$ $\dfrac{8}{7} \times \dfrac{8}{5}$

$\dfrac{5}{8} \times \dfrac{2}{3}$ $\dfrac{8}{5} \times \dfrac{1}{9}$ $\dfrac{3}{8} \times \dfrac{9}{8}$ $\dfrac{7}{6} \times \dfrac{9}{5}$ $\dfrac{5}{8} \times \dfrac{9}{4}$

$\dfrac{6}{5} \times \dfrac{1}{6}$ $\dfrac{5}{4} \times \dfrac{4}{7}$ $\dfrac{3}{2} \times \dfrac{1}{5}$ $\dfrac{1}{6} \times \dfrac{5}{9}$ $\dfrac{3}{2} \times \dfrac{1}{5}$

$\dfrac{5}{7} \times \dfrac{3}{7}$ $\dfrac{1}{9} \times \dfrac{9}{8}$ $\dfrac{3}{2} \times \dfrac{3}{2}$ $\dfrac{8}{7} \times \dfrac{3}{4}$ $\dfrac{5}{3} \times \dfrac{4}{7}$

$\dfrac{7}{9} \times \dfrac{7}{9}$ $\dfrac{9}{5} \times \dfrac{3}{2}$ $\dfrac{7}{6} \times \dfrac{7}{2}$ $\dfrac{1}{8} \times \dfrac{1}{5}$ $\dfrac{1}{3} \times \dfrac{7}{4}$

$\dfrac{8}{5} \times \dfrac{7}{3}$ $\dfrac{3}{7} \times \dfrac{6}{5}$ $\dfrac{9}{8} \times \dfrac{5}{8}$ $\dfrac{9}{7} \times \dfrac{1}{4}$ $\dfrac{2}{5} \times \dfrac{7}{2}$

$\dfrac{3}{5} \times \dfrac{8}{9}$ $\qquad$ $\dfrac{5}{2} \times \dfrac{1}{9}$ $\qquad$ $\dfrac{5}{7} \times \dfrac{1}{9}$ $\qquad$ $\dfrac{5}{6} \times \dfrac{1}{9}$ $\qquad$ $\dfrac{8}{5} \times \dfrac{7}{8}$

$\dfrac{1}{4} \times \dfrac{7}{3}$ $\qquad$ $\dfrac{5}{8} \times \dfrac{1}{6}$ $\qquad$ $\dfrac{9}{4} \times \dfrac{7}{4}$ $\qquad$ $\dfrac{1}{4} \times \dfrac{3}{5}$ $\qquad$ $\dfrac{7}{6} \times \dfrac{9}{4}$

$\dfrac{4}{5} \times \dfrac{4}{7}$ $\qquad$ $\dfrac{3}{7} \times \dfrac{6}{7}$ $\qquad$ $\dfrac{4}{5} \times \dfrac{8}{9}$ $\qquad$ $\dfrac{4}{7} \times \dfrac{9}{4}$ $\qquad$ $\dfrac{8}{9} \times \dfrac{6}{5}$

$\dfrac{1}{5} \times \dfrac{3}{4}$ $\qquad$ $\dfrac{4}{7} \times \dfrac{6}{7}$ $\qquad$ $\dfrac{5}{8} \times \dfrac{6}{5}$ $\qquad$ $\dfrac{4}{9} \times \dfrac{7}{5}$ $\qquad$ $\dfrac{6}{5} \times \dfrac{5}{4}$

$\dfrac{2}{5} \times \dfrac{1}{6}$ $\qquad$ $\dfrac{5}{4} \times \dfrac{2}{5}$ $\qquad$ $\dfrac{9}{5} \times \dfrac{1}{3}$ $\qquad$ $\dfrac{7}{4} \times \dfrac{7}{8}$ $\qquad$ $\dfrac{1}{3} \times \dfrac{5}{9}$

$\frac{2}{5} \times \frac{7}{6}$ $\frac{8}{5} \times \frac{2}{5}$ $\frac{4}{9} \times \frac{7}{2}$ $\frac{1}{2} \times \frac{2}{7}$ $\frac{2}{7} \times \frac{1}{5}$

$\frac{7}{3} \times \frac{2}{7}$ $\frac{3}{2} \times \frac{7}{4}$ $\frac{5}{2} \times \frac{3}{2}$ $\frac{7}{5} \times \frac{1}{4}$ $\frac{1}{7} \times \frac{7}{8}$

$\frac{5}{2} \times \frac{3}{7}$ $\frac{7}{2} \times \frac{8}{5}$ $\frac{4}{7} \times \frac{1}{8}$ $\frac{6}{7} \times \frac{8}{5}$ $\frac{1}{8} \times \frac{8}{5}$

$\frac{2}{3} \times \frac{9}{5}$ $\frac{3}{8} \times \frac{9}{7}$ $\frac{5}{4} \times \frac{9}{2}$ $\frac{4}{3} \times \frac{7}{4}$ $\frac{9}{5} \times \frac{1}{8}$

$\frac{5}{4} \times \frac{8}{3}$ $\frac{5}{3} \times \frac{7}{5}$ $\frac{3}{8} \times \frac{8}{9}$ $\frac{9}{4} \times \frac{9}{5}$ $\frac{4}{7} \times \frac{4}{7}$

$\dfrac{2}{7} \times \dfrac{3}{7}$ $\dfrac{4}{5} \times \dfrac{9}{7}$ $\dfrac{3}{8} \times \dfrac{1}{3}$ $\dfrac{7}{6} \times \dfrac{8}{7}$ $\dfrac{9}{2} \times \dfrac{7}{6}$

$\dfrac{5}{4} \times \dfrac{4}{3}$ $\dfrac{7}{9} \times \dfrac{1}{3}$ $\dfrac{5}{3} \times \dfrac{7}{2}$ $\dfrac{1}{8} \times \dfrac{5}{3}$ $\dfrac{7}{6} \times \dfrac{3}{2}$

$\dfrac{5}{4} \times \dfrac{5}{6}$ $\dfrac{5}{9} \times \dfrac{5}{9}$ $\dfrac{3}{4} \times \dfrac{5}{8}$ $\dfrac{1}{5} \times \dfrac{1}{2}$ $\dfrac{1}{2} \times \dfrac{1}{5}$

$\dfrac{1}{9} \times \dfrac{7}{2}$ $\dfrac{5}{6} \times \dfrac{6}{7}$ $\dfrac{5}{6} \times \dfrac{2}{3}$ $\dfrac{7}{3} \times \dfrac{1}{9}$ $\dfrac{3}{4} \times \dfrac{5}{2}$

$\dfrac{9}{8} \times \dfrac{3}{8}$ $\dfrac{4}{9} \times \dfrac{5}{2}$ $\dfrac{2}{7} \times \dfrac{3}{2}$ $\dfrac{7}{6} \times \dfrac{5}{9}$ $\dfrac{1}{8} \times \dfrac{8}{3}$

$\frac{1}{3} \times \frac{8}{9}$ $\qquad$ $\frac{1}{9} \times \frac{4}{5}$ $\qquad$ $\frac{9}{5} \times \frac{4}{9}$ $\qquad$ $\frac{5}{4} \times \frac{8}{9}$ $\qquad$ $\frac{5}{8} \times \frac{7}{9}$

$\frac{1}{2} \times \frac{1}{3}$ $\qquad$ $\frac{5}{7} \times \frac{5}{2}$ $\qquad$ $\frac{7}{9} \times \frac{8}{7}$ $\qquad$ $\frac{5}{4} \times \frac{9}{7}$ $\qquad$ $\frac{2}{3} \times \frac{5}{2}$

$\frac{8}{7} \times \frac{1}{6}$ $\qquad$ $\frac{3}{5} \times \frac{8}{5}$ $\qquad$ $\frac{8}{7} \times \frac{6}{7}$ $\qquad$ $\frac{1}{7} \times \frac{1}{9}$ $\qquad$ $\frac{4}{7} \times \frac{1}{3}$

$\frac{7}{9} \times \frac{1}{4}$ $\qquad$ $\frac{7}{8} \times \frac{7}{9}$ $\qquad$ $\frac{5}{4} \times \frac{4}{7}$ $\qquad$ $\frac{9}{7} \times \frac{1}{5}$ $\qquad$ $\frac{9}{2} \times \frac{7}{5}$

$\frac{1}{3} \times \frac{1}{6}$ $\qquad$ $\frac{5}{4} \times \frac{9}{5}$ $\qquad$ $\frac{5}{7} \times \frac{5}{6}$ $\qquad$ $\frac{5}{6} \times \frac{5}{3}$ $\qquad$ $\frac{7}{9} \times \frac{9}{2}$

$\dfrac{5}{8} \times \dfrac{6}{5}$ $\dfrac{4}{7} \times \dfrac{3}{5}$ $\dfrac{1}{6} \times \dfrac{7}{4}$ $\dfrac{7}{5} \times \dfrac{5}{8}$ $\dfrac{9}{5} \times \dfrac{1}{8}$

$\dfrac{4}{3} \times \dfrac{8}{7}$ $\dfrac{7}{4} \times \dfrac{4}{5}$ $\dfrac{1}{9} \times \dfrac{7}{5}$ $\dfrac{7}{3} \times \dfrac{8}{7}$ $\dfrac{7}{5} \times \dfrac{6}{5}$

$\dfrac{2}{9} \times \dfrac{9}{8}$ $\dfrac{2}{5} \times \dfrac{8}{3}$ $\dfrac{1}{8} \times \dfrac{9}{8}$ $\dfrac{3}{7} \times \dfrac{3}{2}$ $\dfrac{2}{5} \times \dfrac{7}{2}$

$\dfrac{5}{6} \times \dfrac{1}{9}$ $\dfrac{7}{3} \times \dfrac{5}{4}$ $\dfrac{1}{9} \times \dfrac{1}{9}$ $\dfrac{2}{7} \times \dfrac{9}{7}$ $\dfrac{5}{6} \times \dfrac{4}{5}$

$\dfrac{7}{4} \times \dfrac{7}{9}$ $\dfrac{5}{9} \times \dfrac{9}{2}$ $\dfrac{7}{3} \times \dfrac{7}{8}$ $\dfrac{2}{5} \times \dfrac{3}{4}$ $\dfrac{6}{7} \times \dfrac{2}{9}$

$\frac{5}{3} \times \frac{4}{9}$ $\frac{4}{7} \times \frac{7}{8}$ $\frac{2}{7} \times \frac{9}{7}$ $\frac{5}{8} \times \frac{6}{7}$ $\frac{3}{4} \times \frac{3}{7}$

$\frac{8}{3} \times \frac{3}{5}$ $\frac{5}{8} \times \frac{7}{2}$ $\frac{8}{7} \times \frac{3}{8}$ $\frac{7}{5} \times \frac{3}{4}$ $\frac{8}{5} \times \frac{8}{3}$

$\frac{2}{5} \times \frac{1}{5}$ $\frac{7}{5} \times \frac{4}{7}$ $\frac{3}{2} \times \frac{6}{7}$ $\frac{3}{4} \times \frac{9}{2}$ $\frac{3}{2} \times \frac{7}{3}$

$\frac{7}{3} \times \frac{3}{4}$ $\frac{7}{3} \times \frac{8}{7}$ $\frac{5}{7} \times \frac{1}{8}$ $\frac{8}{9} \times \frac{5}{3}$ $\frac{1}{4} \times \frac{3}{2}$

$\frac{1}{3} \times \frac{1}{9}$ $\frac{9}{2} \times \frac{9}{8}$ $\frac{9}{2} \times \frac{9}{7}$ $\frac{3}{2} \times \frac{5}{9}$ $\frac{4}{7} \times \frac{5}{8}$

$\dfrac{1}{5} \times \dfrac{1}{3}$ $\dfrac{1}{8} \times \dfrac{8}{9}$ $\dfrac{8}{5} \times \dfrac{7}{6}$ $\dfrac{9}{7} \times \dfrac{1}{2}$ $\dfrac{1}{3} \times \dfrac{5}{3}$

$\dfrac{2}{5} \times \dfrac{7}{6}$ $\dfrac{1}{9} \times \dfrac{4}{3}$ $\dfrac{5}{9} \times \dfrac{1}{4}$ $\dfrac{1}{3} \times \dfrac{1}{8}$ $\dfrac{6}{5} \times \dfrac{8}{5}$

$\dfrac{4}{9} \times \dfrac{7}{8}$ $\dfrac{7}{9} \times \dfrac{9}{5}$ $\dfrac{7}{6} \times \dfrac{7}{2}$ $\dfrac{8}{5} \times \dfrac{5}{6}$ $\dfrac{7}{4} \times \dfrac{8}{9}$

$\dfrac{8}{9} \times \dfrac{3}{7}$ $\dfrac{1}{5} \times \dfrac{8}{5}$ $\dfrac{5}{4} \times \dfrac{7}{8}$ $\dfrac{5}{7} \times \dfrac{7}{6}$ $\dfrac{5}{3} \times \dfrac{1}{2}$

$\dfrac{7}{8} \times \dfrac{8}{3}$ $\dfrac{8}{3} \times \dfrac{5}{7}$ $\dfrac{3}{4} \times \dfrac{9}{4}$ $\dfrac{2}{3} \times \dfrac{6}{7}$ $\dfrac{7}{6} \times \dfrac{3}{7}$

$\dfrac{4}{7} \times \dfrac{1}{6}$ $\dfrac{3}{4} \times \dfrac{5}{6}$ $\dfrac{4}{3} \times \dfrac{7}{2}$ $\dfrac{3}{5} \times \dfrac{7}{4}$ $\dfrac{6}{5} \times \dfrac{5}{8}$

$\dfrac{3}{5} \times \dfrac{9}{5}$ $\dfrac{7}{2} \times \dfrac{7}{4}$ $\dfrac{7}{4} \times \dfrac{9}{5}$ $\dfrac{1}{2} \times \dfrac{6}{5}$ $\dfrac{5}{8} \times \dfrac{4}{7}$

$\dfrac{8}{5} \times \dfrac{8}{9}$ $\dfrac{5}{3} \times \dfrac{5}{2}$ $\dfrac{2}{5} \times \dfrac{3}{7}$ $\dfrac{1}{3} \times \dfrac{1}{2}$ $\dfrac{3}{2} \times \dfrac{4}{5}$

$\dfrac{5}{4} \times \dfrac{2}{5}$ $\dfrac{1}{2} \times \dfrac{1}{5}$ $\dfrac{7}{5} \times \dfrac{8}{9}$ $\dfrac{3}{4} \times \dfrac{2}{7}$ $\dfrac{1}{7} \times \dfrac{3}{7}$

$\dfrac{1}{3} \times \dfrac{1}{5}$ $\dfrac{2}{9} \times \dfrac{2}{5}$ $\dfrac{7}{5} \times \dfrac{4}{5}$ $\dfrac{4}{5} \times \dfrac{1}{6}$ $\dfrac{3}{8} \times \dfrac{2}{9}$

$\dfrac{7}{2} \times \dfrac{5}{8}$ $\dfrac{1}{3} \times \dfrac{1}{9}$ $\dfrac{5}{6} \times \dfrac{5}{7}$ $\dfrac{3}{8} \times \dfrac{4}{3}$ $\dfrac{1}{2} \times \dfrac{6}{7}$

$\dfrac{7}{4} \times \dfrac{1}{4}$ $\dfrac{7}{3} \times \dfrac{1}{3}$ $\dfrac{2}{9} \times \dfrac{8}{9}$ $\dfrac{1}{9} \times \dfrac{7}{2}$ $\dfrac{4}{5} \times \dfrac{9}{5}$

$\dfrac{7}{4} \times \dfrac{4}{9}$ $\dfrac{5}{8} \times \dfrac{1}{2}$ $\dfrac{2}{9} \times \dfrac{8}{9}$ $\dfrac{8}{3} \times \dfrac{9}{5}$ $\dfrac{5}{4} \times \dfrac{2}{5}$

$\dfrac{4}{3} \times \dfrac{5}{2}$ $\dfrac{4}{9} \times \dfrac{1}{4}$ $\dfrac{7}{9} \times \dfrac{1}{3}$ $\dfrac{5}{4} \times \dfrac{1}{7}$ $\dfrac{5}{2} \times \dfrac{7}{9}$

$\dfrac{8}{5} \times \dfrac{9}{8}$ $\dfrac{3}{5} \times \dfrac{5}{8}$ $\dfrac{3}{8} \times \dfrac{6}{7}$ $\dfrac{4}{3} \times \dfrac{4}{5}$ $\dfrac{8}{3} \times \dfrac{5}{7}$

$\dfrac{7}{9} \times \dfrac{5}{6}$ $\dfrac{7}{8} \times \dfrac{9}{4}$ $\dfrac{2}{5} \times \dfrac{2}{7}$ $\dfrac{9}{2} \times \dfrac{6}{7}$ $\dfrac{8}{3} \times \dfrac{5}{3}$

$\dfrac{9}{8} \times \dfrac{5}{2}$ $\dfrac{9}{2} \times \dfrac{9}{4}$ $\dfrac{2}{7} \times \dfrac{1}{8}$ $\dfrac{1}{9} \times \dfrac{7}{9}$ $\dfrac{8}{5} \times \dfrac{3}{4}$

$\dfrac{3}{5} \times \dfrac{9}{5}$ $\dfrac{1}{8} \times \dfrac{8}{3}$ $\dfrac{8}{5} \times \dfrac{8}{9}$ $\dfrac{5}{4} \times \dfrac{5}{9}$ $\dfrac{2}{9} \times \dfrac{1}{4}$

$\dfrac{3}{5} \times \dfrac{1}{5}$ $\dfrac{7}{3} \times \dfrac{8}{7}$ $\dfrac{1}{4} \times \dfrac{8}{7}$ $\dfrac{3}{5} \times \dfrac{1}{7}$ $\dfrac{7}{6} \times \dfrac{9}{5}$

$\dfrac{9}{7} \times \dfrac{3}{4}$ $\dfrac{1}{4} \times \dfrac{8}{7}$ $\dfrac{9}{4} \times \dfrac{9}{7}$ $\dfrac{8}{9} \times \dfrac{3}{4}$ $\dfrac{4}{7} \times \dfrac{3}{4}$

$\frac{1}{5} \times \frac{7}{2}$ $\qquad$ $\frac{8}{9} \times \frac{4}{5}$ $\qquad$ $\frac{4}{5} \times \frac{9}{4}$ $\qquad$ $\frac{9}{8} \times \frac{5}{3}$ $\qquad$ $\frac{8}{5} \times \frac{1}{5}$

$\frac{9}{2} \times \frac{7}{4}$ $\qquad$ $\frac{4}{9} \times \frac{4}{7}$ $\qquad$ $\frac{6}{5} \times \frac{4}{5}$ $\qquad$ $\frac{1}{9} \times \frac{3}{4}$ $\qquad$ $\frac{2}{7} \times \frac{2}{3}$

$\frac{5}{3} \times \frac{4}{9}$ $\qquad$ $\frac{5}{4} \times \frac{5}{6}$ $\qquad$ $\frac{7}{3} \times \frac{3}{5}$ $\qquad$ $\frac{8}{3} \times \frac{1}{4}$ $\qquad$ $\frac{3}{4} \times \frac{9}{5}$

$\frac{5}{7} \times \frac{5}{3}$ $\qquad$ $\frac{9}{7} \times \frac{5}{6}$ $\qquad$ $\frac{1}{2} \times \frac{1}{9}$ $\qquad$ $\frac{5}{8} \times \frac{3}{5}$ $\qquad$ $\frac{5}{3} \times \frac{5}{2}$

$\frac{2}{5} \times \frac{8}{9}$ $\qquad$ $\frac{9}{8} \times \frac{7}{8}$ $\qquad$ $\frac{3}{5} \times \frac{8}{7}$ $\qquad$ $\frac{1}{4} \times \frac{3}{4}$ $\qquad$ $\frac{3}{4} \times \frac{7}{6}$

$\frac{5}{3} \times \frac{7}{4}$ $\frac{7}{3} \times \frac{5}{3}$ $\frac{5}{6} \times \frac{1}{7}$ $\frac{7}{4} \times \frac{3}{2}$ $\frac{9}{2} \times \frac{8}{7}$

$\frac{7}{2} \times \frac{4}{5}$ $\frac{7}{4} \times \frac{4}{3}$ $\frac{1}{3} \times \frac{1}{4}$ $\frac{5}{4} \times \frac{9}{4}$ $\frac{7}{5} \times \frac{9}{5}$

$\frac{1}{5} \times \frac{5}{3}$ $\frac{2}{9} \times \frac{5}{6}$ $\frac{1}{5} \times \frac{9}{5}$ $\frac{3}{8} \times \frac{5}{9}$ $\frac{4}{3} \times \frac{8}{5}$

$\frac{2}{3} \times \frac{1}{9}$ $\frac{6}{7} \times \frac{1}{6}$ $\frac{8}{7} \times \frac{1}{6}$ $\frac{4}{5} \times \frac{4}{5}$ $\frac{2}{5} \times \frac{4}{5}$

$\frac{5}{3} \times \frac{1}{4}$ $\frac{7}{2} \times \frac{1}{5}$ $\frac{3}{8} \times \frac{9}{5}$ $\frac{1}{5} \times \frac{3}{7}$ $\frac{7}{2} \times \frac{7}{5}$

$\frac{5}{7} \times \frac{2}{5}$ $\frac{7}{4} \times \frac{6}{7}$ $\frac{3}{5} \times \frac{4}{5}$ $\frac{1}{4} \times \frac{7}{6}$ $\frac{1}{9} \times \frac{3}{2}$

$\frac{4}{7} \times \frac{1}{9}$ $\frac{5}{6} \times \frac{5}{6}$ $\frac{7}{8} \times \frac{9}{2}$ $\frac{7}{8} \times \frac{9}{2}$ $\frac{2}{9} \times \frac{7}{3}$

$\frac{5}{9} \times \frac{2}{5}$ $\frac{5}{2} \times \frac{1}{8}$ $\frac{8}{7} \times \frac{1}{5}$ $\frac{7}{4} \times \frac{5}{6}$ $\frac{8}{9} \times \frac{3}{8}$

$\frac{5}{7} \times \frac{7}{9}$ $\frac{1}{9} \times \frac{6}{5}$ $\frac{1}{6} \times \frac{1}{2}$ $\frac{5}{3} \times \frac{5}{4}$ $\frac{3}{7} \times \frac{5}{4}$

$\frac{1}{3} \times \frac{7}{5}$ $\frac{1}{4} \times \frac{7}{2}$ $\frac{1}{5} \times \frac{4}{3}$ $\frac{9}{8} \times \frac{1}{9}$ $\frac{9}{8} \times \frac{5}{4}$

$\frac{1}{7} \times \frac{2}{5}$ $\qquad$ $\frac{5}{2} \times \frac{7}{5}$ $\qquad$ $\frac{4}{3} \times \frac{1}{7}$ $\qquad$ $\frac{5}{3} \times \frac{7}{3}$ $\qquad$ $\frac{1}{4} \times \frac{5}{7}$

$\frac{6}{7} \times \frac{7}{9}$ $\qquad$ $\frac{3}{2} \times \frac{9}{7}$ $\qquad$ $\frac{3}{8} \times \frac{6}{7}$ $\qquad$ $\frac{1}{6} \times \frac{3}{2}$ $\qquad$ $\frac{7}{4} \times \frac{1}{8}$

$\frac{2}{3} \times \frac{9}{5}$ $\qquad$ $\frac{9}{2} \times \frac{2}{7}$ $\qquad$ $\frac{7}{3} \times \frac{6}{5}$ $\qquad$ $\frac{8}{5} \times \frac{2}{9}$ $\qquad$ $\frac{4}{7} \times \frac{1}{5}$

$\frac{5}{3} \times \frac{4}{3}$ $\qquad$ $\frac{7}{2} \times \frac{7}{5}$ $\qquad$ $\frac{2}{9} \times \frac{1}{3}$ $\qquad$ $\frac{9}{5} \times \frac{7}{2}$ $\qquad$ $\frac{4}{5} \times \frac{5}{8}$

$\frac{9}{2} \times \frac{7}{9}$ $\qquad$ $\frac{1}{5} \times \frac{9}{8}$ $\qquad$ $\frac{1}{5} \times \frac{9}{2}$ $\qquad$ $\frac{3}{8} \times \frac{8}{9}$ $\qquad$ $\frac{1}{8} \times \frac{3}{8}$

$\dfrac{3}{5} \times \dfrac{9}{7}$ $\qquad$ $\dfrac{9}{8} \times \dfrac{9}{2}$ $\qquad$ $\dfrac{1}{4} \times \dfrac{2}{3}$ $\qquad$ $\dfrac{9}{4} \times \dfrac{7}{2}$ $\qquad$ $\dfrac{5}{4} \times \dfrac{5}{7}$

$\dfrac{3}{2} \times \dfrac{5}{3}$ $\qquad$ $\dfrac{2}{7} \times \dfrac{1}{7}$ $\qquad$ $\dfrac{9}{2} \times \dfrac{1}{5}$ $\qquad$ $\dfrac{7}{6} \times \dfrac{4}{9}$ $\qquad$ $\dfrac{5}{8} \times \dfrac{7}{2}$

$\dfrac{4}{3} \times \dfrac{9}{7}$ $\qquad$ $\dfrac{9}{7} \times \dfrac{5}{9}$ $\qquad$ $\dfrac{1}{3} \times \dfrac{1}{4}$ $\qquad$ $\dfrac{7}{6} \times \dfrac{3}{2}$ $\qquad$ $\dfrac{4}{5} \times \dfrac{5}{9}$

$\dfrac{6}{7} \times \dfrac{7}{4}$ $\qquad$ $\dfrac{3}{2} \times \dfrac{2}{9}$ $\qquad$ $\dfrac{1}{9} \times \dfrac{3}{7}$ $\qquad$ $\dfrac{9}{8} \times \dfrac{1}{6}$ $\qquad$ $\dfrac{7}{9} \times \dfrac{2}{9}$

$\dfrac{2}{7} \times \dfrac{7}{8}$ $\qquad$ $\dfrac{4}{9} \times \dfrac{9}{8}$ $\qquad$ $\dfrac{6}{7} \times \dfrac{3}{5}$ $\qquad$ $\dfrac{5}{3} \times \dfrac{4}{9}$ $\qquad$ $\dfrac{5}{3} \times \dfrac{8}{9}$

$\dfrac{2}{9} \times \dfrac{6}{5}$ $\dfrac{7}{4} \times \dfrac{5}{3}$ $\dfrac{7}{3} \times \dfrac{3}{8}$ $\dfrac{9}{2} \times \dfrac{1}{2}$ $\dfrac{7}{9} \times \dfrac{3}{7}$

$\dfrac{5}{7} \times \dfrac{9}{4}$ $\dfrac{4}{9} \times \dfrac{7}{5}$ $\dfrac{9}{7} \times \dfrac{7}{4}$ $\dfrac{2}{5} \times \dfrac{9}{4}$ $\dfrac{2}{9} \times \dfrac{8}{7}$

$\dfrac{7}{2} \times \dfrac{7}{3}$ $\dfrac{3}{4} \times \dfrac{1}{7}$ $\dfrac{7}{2} \times \dfrac{5}{7}$ $\dfrac{7}{9} \times \dfrac{1}{3}$ $\dfrac{5}{7} \times \dfrac{7}{2}$

$\dfrac{5}{3} \times \dfrac{4}{9}$ $\dfrac{7}{3} \times \dfrac{2}{3}$ $\dfrac{1}{3} \times \dfrac{7}{9}$ $\dfrac{1}{8} \times \dfrac{4}{3}$ $\dfrac{2}{3} \times \dfrac{5}{3}$

$\dfrac{1}{6} \times \dfrac{7}{8}$ $\dfrac{9}{4} \times \dfrac{7}{2}$ $\dfrac{7}{6} \times \dfrac{4}{7}$ $\dfrac{1}{3} \times \dfrac{1}{5}$ $\dfrac{5}{8} \times \dfrac{3}{8}$

$\dfrac{9}{5} \times \dfrac{1}{5}$ $\dfrac{9}{7} \times \dfrac{2}{7}$ $\dfrac{2}{3} \times \dfrac{5}{6}$ $\dfrac{5}{8} \times \dfrac{5}{4}$ $\dfrac{8}{7} \times \dfrac{4}{7}$

$\dfrac{2}{5} \times \dfrac{7}{9}$ $\dfrac{5}{8} \times \dfrac{9}{5}$ $\dfrac{1}{4} \times \dfrac{3}{8}$ $\dfrac{5}{9} \times \dfrac{5}{4}$ $\dfrac{8}{5} \times \dfrac{3}{4}$

$\dfrac{7}{4} \times \dfrac{6}{5}$ $\dfrac{2}{3} \times \dfrac{2}{3}$ $\dfrac{1}{4} \times \dfrac{5}{4}$ $\dfrac{5}{6} \times \dfrac{1}{7}$ $\dfrac{2}{9} \times \dfrac{1}{4}$

$\dfrac{8}{7} \times \dfrac{7}{9}$ $\dfrac{3}{8} \times \dfrac{3}{7}$ $\dfrac{2}{5} \times \dfrac{1}{2}$ $\dfrac{7}{4} \times \dfrac{8}{9}$ $\dfrac{1}{9} \times \dfrac{9}{8}$

$\dfrac{8}{9} \times \dfrac{1}{7}$ $\dfrac{7}{4} \times \dfrac{6}{7}$ $\dfrac{5}{7} \times \dfrac{3}{4}$ $\dfrac{3}{8} \times \dfrac{5}{6}$ $\dfrac{5}{6} \times \dfrac{7}{5}$

$\dfrac{2}{9} \times \dfrac{4}{5}$ $\dfrac{7}{9} \times \dfrac{2}{9}$ $\dfrac{1}{8} \times \dfrac{1}{3}$ $\dfrac{1}{6} \times \dfrac{6}{5}$ $\dfrac{7}{3} \times \dfrac{5}{3}$

$\dfrac{7}{9} \times \dfrac{1}{3}$ $\dfrac{9}{8} \times \dfrac{6}{7}$ $\dfrac{2}{5} \times \dfrac{7}{2}$ $\dfrac{1}{8} \times \dfrac{2}{7}$ $\dfrac{3}{7} \times \dfrac{7}{4}$

$\dfrac{7}{9} \times \dfrac{1}{3}$ $\dfrac{7}{2} \times \dfrac{5}{6}$ $\dfrac{1}{4} \times \dfrac{5}{2}$ $\dfrac{1}{8} \times \dfrac{7}{3}$ $\dfrac{1}{6} \times \dfrac{8}{5}$

$\dfrac{6}{7} \times \dfrac{3}{2}$ $\dfrac{5}{7} \times \dfrac{9}{4}$ $\dfrac{1}{5} \times \dfrac{7}{4}$ $\dfrac{1}{8} \times \dfrac{2}{9}$ $\dfrac{3}{4} \times \dfrac{7}{9}$

$\dfrac{1}{7} \times \dfrac{1}{6}$ $\dfrac{4}{5} \times \dfrac{6}{5}$ $\dfrac{2}{7} \times \dfrac{7}{6}$ $\dfrac{3}{5} \times \dfrac{1}{6}$ $\dfrac{9}{5} \times \dfrac{9}{2}$

Part 4: Practice Dividing Fractions

To divide two fractions, first reciprocate the second fraction and then multiply the first fraction with the reciprocated second fraction. To find the reciprocal of a fraction, just trade the numerator and denominator.

EXAMPLES

$$\frac{3}{4} \div \frac{1}{2}$$

$$= \frac{3}{4} \times \frac{2}{1}$$

$$= \frac{3 \cdot 2}{4 \cdot 1}$$

$$= \frac{6}{4}$$

$$= \frac{3}{2}$$

$$\frac{5}{6} \div \frac{2}{3}$$

$$= \frac{5}{6} \times \frac{3}{2}$$

$$= \frac{5 \cdot 3}{6 \cdot 2}$$

$$= \frac{15}{12}$$

$$= \frac{5}{4}$$

$\frac{7}{9} \div \frac{3}{8}$ $\frac{4}{9} \div \frac{5}{9}$ $\frac{1}{8} \div \frac{9}{2}$ $\frac{5}{7} \div \frac{5}{2}$ $\frac{8}{3} \div \frac{1}{7}$

$\frac{6}{7} \div \frac{4}{9}$ $\frac{1}{8} \div \frac{2}{5}$ $\frac{1}{3} \div \frac{1}{8}$ $\frac{9}{4} \div \frac{6}{7}$ $\frac{2}{7} \div \frac{7}{9}$

$\frac{5}{7} \div \frac{2}{3}$ $\frac{7}{4} \div \frac{6}{5}$ $\frac{1}{4} \div \frac{3}{8}$ $\frac{5}{4} \div \frac{5}{6}$ $\frac{8}{9} \div \frac{6}{7}$

$\frac{3}{2} \div \frac{7}{2}$ $\frac{9}{7} \div \frac{1}{5}$ $\frac{6}{5} \div \frac{5}{9}$ $\frac{1}{9} \div \frac{1}{2}$ $\frac{7}{4} \div \frac{1}{6}$

$\frac{5}{8} \div \frac{3}{4}$ $\frac{1}{3} \div \frac{7}{9}$ $\frac{7}{4} \div \frac{4}{9}$ $\frac{5}{4} \div \frac{8}{7}$ $\frac{1}{6} \div \frac{8}{3}$

$\dfrac{2}{9} \div \dfrac{7}{4}$ $\dfrac{5}{9} \div \dfrac{1}{6}$ $\dfrac{7}{9} \div \dfrac{4}{9}$ $\dfrac{5}{9} \div \dfrac{3}{5}$ $\dfrac{5}{4} \div \dfrac{3}{7}$

$\dfrac{8}{7} \div \dfrac{3}{4}$ $\dfrac{1}{4} \div \dfrac{6}{5}$ $\dfrac{9}{2} \div \dfrac{4}{9}$ $\dfrac{8}{3} \div \dfrac{9}{5}$ $\dfrac{8}{9} \div \dfrac{7}{8}$

$\dfrac{1}{3} \div \dfrac{7}{4}$ $\dfrac{7}{4} \div \dfrac{6}{7}$ $\dfrac{9}{8} \div \dfrac{9}{7}$ $\dfrac{1}{7} \div \dfrac{6}{5}$ $\dfrac{9}{5} \div \dfrac{4}{7}$

$\dfrac{5}{7} \div \dfrac{9}{4}$ $\dfrac{9}{4} \div \dfrac{9}{5}$ $\dfrac{4}{9} \div \dfrac{5}{6}$ $\dfrac{5}{7} \div \dfrac{1}{4}$ $\dfrac{9}{8} \div \dfrac{7}{5}$

$\dfrac{3}{7} \div \dfrac{7}{4}$ $\dfrac{3}{8} \div \dfrac{5}{6}$ $\dfrac{5}{2} \div \dfrac{3}{7}$ $\dfrac{3}{4} \div \dfrac{4}{9}$ $\dfrac{5}{6} \div \dfrac{7}{3}$

$\frac{4}{5} \div \frac{1}{7}$ $\qquad$ $\frac{1}{2} \div \frac{2}{9}$ $\qquad$ $\frac{1}{2} \div \frac{7}{2}$ $\qquad$ $\frac{2}{9} \div \frac{3}{7}$ $\qquad$ $\frac{3}{2} \div \frac{7}{9}$

$\frac{9}{7} \div \frac{4}{5}$ $\qquad$ $\frac{1}{5} \div \frac{6}{7}$ $\qquad$ $\frac{5}{8} \div \frac{1}{2}$ $\qquad$ $\frac{5}{6} \div \frac{3}{2}$ $\qquad$ $\frac{7}{5} \div \frac{5}{2}$

$\frac{1}{8} \div \frac{7}{8}$ $\qquad$ $\frac{2}{9} \div \frac{2}{5}$ $\qquad$ $\frac{7}{4} \div \frac{2}{9}$ $\qquad$ $\frac{6}{7} \div \frac{4}{9}$ $\qquad$ $\frac{2}{3} \div \frac{3}{8}$

$\frac{6}{5} \div \frac{2}{9}$ $\qquad$ $\frac{1}{7} \div \frac{4}{3}$ $\qquad$ $\frac{1}{3} \div \frac{4}{3}$ $\qquad$ $\frac{1}{3} \div \frac{9}{8}$ $\qquad$ $\frac{5}{8} \div \frac{8}{5}$

$\frac{1}{5} \div \frac{5}{9}$ $\qquad$ $\frac{7}{4} \div \frac{1}{5}$ $\qquad$ $\frac{2}{7} \div \frac{8}{3}$ $\qquad$ $\frac{9}{7} \div \frac{5}{6}$ $\qquad$ $\frac{5}{3} \div \frac{7}{3}$

$\dfrac{4}{7} \div \dfrac{1}{8}$ $\qquad$ $\dfrac{3}{4} \div \dfrac{7}{4}$ $\qquad$ $\dfrac{1}{7} \div \dfrac{6}{5}$ $\qquad$ $\dfrac{9}{4} \div \dfrac{7}{6}$ $\qquad$ $\dfrac{9}{5} \div \dfrac{2}{3}$

$\dfrac{7}{6} \div \dfrac{5}{7}$ $\qquad$ $\dfrac{5}{8} \div \dfrac{5}{7}$ $\qquad$ $\dfrac{1}{8} \div \dfrac{3}{4}$ $\qquad$ $\dfrac{4}{7} \div \dfrac{1}{8}$ $\qquad$ $\dfrac{9}{2} \div \dfrac{7}{6}$

$\dfrac{1}{2} \div \dfrac{7}{5}$ $\qquad$ $\dfrac{5}{7} \div \dfrac{7}{5}$ $\qquad$ $\dfrac{6}{5} \div \dfrac{3}{4}$ $\qquad$ $\dfrac{8}{9} \div \dfrac{1}{4}$ $\qquad$ $\dfrac{3}{8} \div \dfrac{8}{7}$

$\dfrac{1}{2} \div \dfrac{7}{5}$ $\qquad$ $\dfrac{2}{5} \div \dfrac{1}{2}$ $\qquad$ $\dfrac{7}{5} \div \dfrac{5}{3}$ $\qquad$ $\dfrac{9}{7} \div \dfrac{2}{7}$ $\qquad$ $\dfrac{2}{9} \div \dfrac{3}{2}$

$\dfrac{1}{6} \div \dfrac{3}{4}$ $\qquad$ $\dfrac{9}{2} \div \dfrac{8}{7}$ $\qquad$ $\dfrac{3}{5} \div \dfrac{9}{5}$ $\qquad$ $\dfrac{5}{4} \div \dfrac{9}{4}$ $\qquad$ $\dfrac{1}{4} \div \dfrac{8}{5}$

$\dfrac{1}{4} \div \dfrac{1}{3}$ $\dfrac{1}{4} \div \dfrac{2}{3}$ $\dfrac{3}{2} \div \dfrac{7}{8}$ $\dfrac{3}{8} \div \dfrac{5}{4}$ $\dfrac{1}{2} \div \dfrac{5}{6}$

$\dfrac{7}{5} \div \dfrac{1}{9}$ $\dfrac{2}{9} \div \dfrac{7}{6}$ $\dfrac{7}{9} \div \dfrac{5}{7}$ $\dfrac{3}{4} \div \dfrac{5}{6}$ $\dfrac{1}{7} \div \dfrac{9}{5}$

$\dfrac{5}{9} \div \dfrac{1}{7}$ $\dfrac{9}{7} \div \dfrac{2}{3}$ $\dfrac{7}{8} \div \dfrac{3}{4}$ $\dfrac{4}{7} \div \dfrac{7}{6}$ $\dfrac{9}{5} \div \dfrac{5}{2}$

$\dfrac{8}{5} \div \dfrac{2}{7}$ $\dfrac{4}{7} \div \dfrac{6}{7}$ $\dfrac{3}{4} \div \dfrac{9}{5}$ $\dfrac{3}{2} \div \dfrac{7}{5}$ $\dfrac{7}{2} \div \dfrac{5}{3}$

$\dfrac{9}{7} \div \dfrac{1}{8}$ $\dfrac{3}{2} \div \dfrac{5}{6}$ $\dfrac{5}{3} \div \dfrac{1}{5}$ $\dfrac{5}{9} \div \dfrac{7}{3}$ $\dfrac{1}{8} \div \dfrac{7}{8}$

$$\frac{7}{6} \div \frac{3}{2} \qquad \frac{7}{8} \div \frac{6}{7} \qquad \frac{8}{7} \div \frac{8}{3} \qquad \frac{5}{9} \div \frac{1}{2} \qquad \frac{1}{7} \div \frac{7}{8}$$

$$\frac{5}{3} \div \frac{4}{9} \qquad \frac{1}{3} \div \frac{8}{3} \qquad \frac{8}{7} \div \frac{4}{3} \qquad \frac{6}{5} \div \frac{5}{6} \qquad \frac{8}{7} \div \frac{1}{5}$$

$$\frac{8}{7} \div \frac{8}{3} \qquad \frac{7}{8} \div \frac{4}{9} \qquad \frac{4}{9} \div \frac{3}{4} \qquad \frac{7}{4} \div \frac{3}{8} \qquad \frac{1}{9} \div \frac{3}{4}$$

$$\frac{7}{8} \div \frac{1}{4} \qquad \frac{3}{4} \div \frac{2}{5} \qquad \frac{7}{4} \div \frac{1}{7} \qquad \frac{7}{6} \div \frac{5}{7} \qquad \frac{8}{9} \div \frac{7}{6}$$

$$\frac{3}{5} \div \frac{6}{5} \qquad \frac{4}{9} \div \frac{2}{7} \qquad \frac{8}{9} \div \frac{8}{5} \qquad \frac{7}{3} \div \frac{7}{4} \qquad \frac{7}{6} \div \frac{6}{5}$$

$\frac{2}{3} \div \frac{4}{7}$ $\frac{6}{5} \div \frac{7}{4}$ $\frac{3}{8} \div \frac{5}{4}$ $\frac{5}{8} \div \frac{2}{7}$ $\frac{1}{6} \div \frac{2}{3}$

$\frac{9}{7} \div \frac{9}{8}$ $\frac{9}{2} \div \frac{4}{7}$ $\frac{9}{4} \div \frac{5}{6}$ $\frac{3}{7} \div \frac{1}{5}$ $\frac{1}{8} \div \frac{6}{7}$

$\frac{4}{9} \div \frac{7}{5}$ $\frac{7}{6} \div \frac{5}{3}$ $\frac{1}{2} \div \frac{1}{9}$ $\frac{1}{5} \div \frac{6}{7}$ $\frac{5}{2} \div \frac{7}{6}$

$\frac{5}{3} \div \frac{2}{7}$ $\frac{9}{2} \div \frac{4}{7}$ $\frac{5}{9} \div \frac{9}{2}$ $\frac{7}{4} \div \frac{5}{8}$ $\frac{9}{4} \div \frac{8}{9}$

$\frac{4}{3} \div \frac{9}{8}$ $\frac{3}{4} \div \frac{5}{3}$ $\frac{1}{9} \div \frac{7}{3}$ $\frac{8}{7} \div \frac{5}{6}$ $\frac{7}{8} \div \frac{7}{2}$

$$\frac{4}{5} \div \frac{1}{4} \qquad \frac{2}{7} \div \frac{1}{6} \qquad \frac{6}{7} \div \frac{7}{9} \qquad \frac{1}{4} \div \frac{9}{8} \qquad \frac{1}{3} \div \frac{2}{5}$$

$$\frac{8}{5} \div \frac{5}{4} \qquad \frac{1}{8} \div \frac{5}{9} \qquad \frac{2}{5} \div \frac{1}{9} \qquad \frac{7}{3} \div \frac{1}{8} \qquad \frac{1}{8} \div \frac{6}{7}$$

$$\frac{4}{3} \div \frac{8}{9} \qquad \frac{3}{7} \div \frac{2}{7} \qquad \frac{5}{8} \div \frac{8}{5} \qquad \frac{4}{7} \div \frac{2}{9} \qquad \frac{3}{7} \div \frac{8}{9}$$

$$\frac{8}{3} \div \frac{9}{7} \qquad \frac{9}{7} \div \frac{5}{7} \qquad \frac{7}{5} \div \frac{5}{3} \qquad \frac{1}{7} \div \frac{5}{4} \qquad \frac{8}{3} \div \frac{7}{8}$$

$$\frac{2}{7} \div \frac{7}{9} \qquad \frac{2}{3} \div \frac{1}{7} \qquad \frac{6}{7} \div \frac{3}{5} \qquad \frac{1}{9} \div \frac{4}{5} \qquad \frac{7}{9} \div \frac{8}{9}$$

$\frac{8}{9} \div \frac{1}{4}$ $\frac{3}{7} \div \frac{6}{7}$ $\frac{3}{2} \div \frac{9}{8}$ $\frac{1}{6} \div \frac{9}{4}$ $\frac{2}{3} \div \frac{9}{4}$

$\frac{1}{5} \div \frac{9}{2}$ $\frac{4}{9} \div \frac{7}{3}$ $\frac{7}{3} \div \frac{2}{5}$ $\frac{1}{3} \div \frac{4}{9}$ $\frac{1}{9} \div \frac{1}{5}$

$\frac{3}{4} \div \frac{1}{3}$ $\frac{1}{7} \div \frac{7}{5}$ $\frac{3}{2} \div \frac{2}{5}$ $\frac{5}{9} \div \frac{3}{2}$ $\frac{1}{9} \div \frac{5}{3}$

$\frac{5}{4} \div \frac{5}{9}$ $\frac{7}{6} \div \frac{6}{7}$ $\frac{8}{5} \div \frac{6}{7}$ $\frac{1}{9} \div \frac{9}{7}$ $\frac{8}{7} \div \frac{1}{9}$

$\frac{9}{4} \div \frac{1}{9}$ $\frac{7}{2} \div \frac{3}{2}$ $\frac{1}{8} \div \frac{1}{7}$ $\frac{9}{5} \div \frac{6}{5}$ $\frac{9}{7} \div \frac{4}{3}$

$\dfrac{6}{7} \div \dfrac{7}{9}$ $\dfrac{7}{6} \div \dfrac{3}{5}$ $\dfrac{1}{5} \div \dfrac{7}{3}$ $\dfrac{9}{7} \div \dfrac{3}{4}$ $\dfrac{9}{2} \div \dfrac{5}{3}$

$\dfrac{4}{9} \div \dfrac{5}{6}$ $\dfrac{8}{7} \div \dfrac{2}{9}$ $\dfrac{4}{7} \div \dfrac{9}{5}$ $\dfrac{7}{8} \div \dfrac{5}{2}$ $\dfrac{5}{4} \div \dfrac{8}{7}$

$\dfrac{5}{3} \div \dfrac{5}{8}$ $\dfrac{7}{9} \div \dfrac{1}{5}$ $\dfrac{1}{9} \div \dfrac{2}{9}$ $\dfrac{1}{2} \div \dfrac{4}{7}$ $\dfrac{7}{5} \div \dfrac{9}{7}$

$\dfrac{4}{5} \div \dfrac{5}{2}$ $\dfrac{7}{3} \div \dfrac{5}{4}$ $\dfrac{9}{7} \div \dfrac{1}{2}$ $\dfrac{5}{9} \div \dfrac{4}{7}$ $\dfrac{9}{8} \div \dfrac{5}{6}$

$\dfrac{9}{5} \div \dfrac{2}{5}$ $\dfrac{4}{3} \div \dfrac{1}{8}$ $\dfrac{1}{6} \div \dfrac{7}{3}$ $\dfrac{3}{2} \div \dfrac{9}{4}$ $\dfrac{1}{6} \div \dfrac{1}{3}$

$\dfrac{9}{7} \div \dfrac{1}{4}$ $\qquad$ $\dfrac{8}{5} \div \dfrac{5}{7}$ $\qquad$ $\dfrac{1}{7} \div \dfrac{9}{2}$ $\qquad$ $\dfrac{1}{4} \div \dfrac{5}{6}$ $\qquad$ $\dfrac{5}{4} \div \dfrac{3}{5}$

$\dfrac{7}{3} \div \dfrac{8}{3}$ $\qquad$ $\dfrac{5}{9} \div \dfrac{1}{3}$ $\qquad$ $\dfrac{5}{6} \div \dfrac{8}{7}$ $\qquad$ $\dfrac{7}{8} \div \dfrac{5}{7}$ $\qquad$ $\dfrac{5}{8} \div \dfrac{2}{5}$

$\dfrac{1}{8} \div \dfrac{9}{8}$ $\qquad$ $\dfrac{9}{2} \div \dfrac{4}{7}$ $\qquad$ $\dfrac{1}{9} \div \dfrac{8}{3}$ $\qquad$ $\dfrac{1}{6} \div \dfrac{3}{2}$ $\qquad$ $\dfrac{5}{3} \div \dfrac{5}{8}$

$\dfrac{6}{5} \div \dfrac{5}{6}$ $\qquad$ $\dfrac{1}{5} \div \dfrac{5}{8}$ $\qquad$ $\dfrac{2}{7} \div \dfrac{5}{7}$ $\qquad$ $\dfrac{8}{9} \div \dfrac{9}{7}$ $\qquad$ $\dfrac{5}{4} \div \dfrac{4}{9}$

$\dfrac{4}{3} \div \dfrac{9}{5}$ $\qquad$ $\dfrac{1}{6} \div \dfrac{4}{3}$ $\qquad$ $\dfrac{3}{7} \div \dfrac{6}{7}$ $\qquad$ $\dfrac{9}{7} \div \dfrac{5}{9}$ $\qquad$ $\dfrac{7}{9} \div \dfrac{8}{7}$

$$\frac{5}{2} \div \frac{6}{7} \qquad \frac{3}{4} \div \frac{5}{7} \qquad \frac{5}{8} \div \frac{3}{5} \qquad \frac{7}{6} \div \frac{8}{7} \qquad \frac{1}{6} \div \frac{3}{5}$$

$$\frac{3}{4} \div \frac{3}{7} \qquad \frac{4}{3} \div \frac{4}{7} \qquad \frac{3}{8} \div \frac{7}{2} \qquad \frac{7}{4} \div \frac{5}{3} \qquad \frac{7}{9} \div \frac{9}{4}$$

$$\frac{6}{7} \div \frac{7}{8} \qquad \frac{1}{4} \div \frac{3}{4} \qquad \frac{1}{7} \div \frac{5}{9} \qquad \frac{7}{3} \div \frac{1}{8} \qquad \frac{5}{3} \div \frac{3}{7}$$

$$\frac{5}{4} \div \frac{6}{7} \qquad \frac{4}{5} \div \frac{5}{8} \qquad \frac{5}{7} \div \frac{7}{9} \qquad \frac{8}{9} \div \frac{7}{4} \qquad \frac{3}{2} \div \frac{7}{2}$$

$$\frac{2}{9} \div \frac{7}{4} \qquad \frac{4}{7} \div \frac{6}{7} \qquad \frac{7}{5} \div \frac{7}{3} \qquad \frac{5}{3} \div \frac{1}{7} \qquad \frac{1}{3} \div \frac{5}{6}$$

$\frac{1}{7} \div \frac{2}{9}$ $\frac{1}{9} \div \frac{7}{9}$ $\frac{4}{7} \div \frac{9}{7}$ $\frac{5}{2} \div \frac{5}{3}$ $\frac{9}{8} \div \frac{4}{5}$

$\frac{3}{5} \div \frac{2}{7}$ $\frac{2}{5} \div \frac{5}{7}$ $\frac{7}{5} \div \frac{2}{9}$ $\frac{7}{9} \div \frac{2}{5}$ $\frac{8}{9} \div \frac{8}{3}$

$\frac{9}{5} \div \frac{3}{8}$ $\frac{3}{4} \div \frac{5}{8}$ $\frac{2}{5} \div \frac{6}{5}$ $\frac{4}{7} \div \frac{6}{7}$ $\frac{8}{9} \div \frac{7}{5}$

$\frac{2}{5} \div \frac{7}{9}$ $\frac{3}{4} \div \frac{3}{2}$ $\frac{7}{6} \div \frac{7}{5}$ $\frac{4}{7} \div \frac{2}{9}$ $\frac{6}{5} \div \frac{2}{3}$

$\frac{9}{4} \div \frac{8}{3}$ $\frac{7}{5} \div \frac{1}{7}$ $\frac{7}{4} \div \frac{2}{5}$ $\frac{1}{4} \div \frac{8}{5}$ $\frac{1}{5} \div \frac{1}{7}$

$\dfrac{9}{4} \div \dfrac{9}{5}$ $\qquad$ $\dfrac{8}{9} \div \dfrac{7}{3}$ $\qquad$ $\dfrac{1}{3} \div \dfrac{9}{5}$ $\qquad$ $\dfrac{4}{3} \div \dfrac{3}{8}$ $\qquad$ $\dfrac{2}{9} \div \dfrac{5}{8}$

$\dfrac{4}{9} \div \dfrac{1}{2}$ $\qquad$ $\dfrac{5}{6} \div \dfrac{9}{5}$ $\qquad$ $\dfrac{1}{6} \div \dfrac{1}{2}$ $\qquad$ $\dfrac{2}{3} \div \dfrac{8}{3}$ $\qquad$ $\dfrac{4}{5} \div \dfrac{1}{2}$

$\dfrac{7}{5} \div \dfrac{3}{4}$ $\qquad$ $\dfrac{6}{7} \div \dfrac{1}{3}$ $\qquad$ $\dfrac{7}{4} \div \dfrac{4}{3}$ $\qquad$ $\dfrac{1}{9} \div \dfrac{7}{8}$ $\qquad$ $\dfrac{5}{9} \div \dfrac{1}{2}$

$\dfrac{5}{9} \div \dfrac{8}{3}$ $\qquad$ $\dfrac{8}{3} \div \dfrac{7}{5}$ $\qquad$ $\dfrac{8}{5} \div \dfrac{1}{3}$ $\qquad$ $\dfrac{7}{6} \div \dfrac{6}{7}$ $\qquad$ $\dfrac{3}{5} \div \dfrac{4}{3}$

$\dfrac{1}{8} \div \dfrac{7}{4}$ $\qquad$ $\dfrac{1}{4} \div \dfrac{3}{2}$ $\qquad$ $\dfrac{5}{9} \div \dfrac{2}{9}$ $\qquad$ $\dfrac{1}{8} \div \dfrac{1}{4}$ $\qquad$ $\dfrac{9}{8} \div \dfrac{7}{5}$

$\dfrac{7}{5} \div \dfrac{4}{9}$ $\dfrac{7}{5} \div \dfrac{4}{9}$ $\dfrac{9}{2} \div \dfrac{7}{6}$ $\dfrac{5}{3} \div \dfrac{3}{8}$ $\dfrac{7}{8} \div \dfrac{3}{2}$

$\dfrac{3}{4} \div \dfrac{3}{7}$ $\dfrac{6}{7} \div \dfrac{4}{3}$ $\dfrac{7}{4} \div \dfrac{7}{3}$ $\dfrac{8}{9} \div \dfrac{1}{2}$ $\dfrac{8}{9} \div \dfrac{8}{3}$

$\dfrac{6}{5} \div \dfrac{1}{9}$ $\dfrac{7}{4} \div \dfrac{6}{5}$ $\dfrac{5}{9} \div \dfrac{4}{3}$ $\dfrac{3}{5} \div \dfrac{5}{4}$ $\dfrac{7}{6} \div \dfrac{7}{4}$

$\dfrac{1}{7} \div \dfrac{7}{9}$ $\dfrac{3}{4} \div \dfrac{5}{9}$ $\dfrac{7}{6} \div \dfrac{8}{5}$ $\dfrac{7}{4} \div \dfrac{7}{9}$ $\dfrac{4}{3} \div \dfrac{5}{7}$

$\dfrac{9}{4} \div \dfrac{4}{3}$ $\dfrac{3}{7} \div \dfrac{5}{4}$ $\dfrac{3}{5} \div \dfrac{7}{6}$ $\dfrac{7}{4} \div \dfrac{9}{8}$ $\dfrac{5}{6} \div \dfrac{1}{5}$

$\dfrac{6}{7} \div \dfrac{5}{4}$ $\qquad$ $\dfrac{7}{5} \div \dfrac{2}{7}$ $\qquad$ $\dfrac{7}{4} \div \dfrac{3}{7}$ $\qquad$ $\dfrac{7}{5} \div \dfrac{4}{9}$ $\qquad$ $\dfrac{1}{2} \div \dfrac{3}{4}$

$\dfrac{5}{2} \div \dfrac{4}{5}$ $\qquad$ $\dfrac{7}{3} \div \dfrac{7}{8}$ $\qquad$ $\dfrac{4}{3} \div \dfrac{3}{8}$ $\qquad$ $\dfrac{9}{7} \div \dfrac{7}{5}$ $\qquad$ $\dfrac{1}{3} \div \dfrac{6}{5}$

$\dfrac{5}{6} \div \dfrac{4}{5}$ $\qquad$ $\dfrac{2}{3} \div \dfrac{7}{6}$ $\qquad$ $\dfrac{5}{7} \div \dfrac{9}{2}$ $\qquad$ $\dfrac{9}{5} \div \dfrac{5}{4}$ $\qquad$ $\dfrac{3}{2} \div \dfrac{2}{7}$

$\dfrac{8}{7} \div \dfrac{1}{8}$ $\qquad$ $\dfrac{5}{8} \div \dfrac{1}{5}$ $\qquad$ $\dfrac{8}{7} \div \dfrac{7}{9}$ $\qquad$ $\dfrac{9}{7} \div \dfrac{9}{5}$ $\qquad$ $\dfrac{1}{2} \div \dfrac{9}{8}$

$\dfrac{7}{4} \div \dfrac{7}{3}$ $\qquad$ $\dfrac{9}{2} \div \dfrac{5}{9}$ $\qquad$ $\dfrac{9}{4} \div \dfrac{5}{2}$ $\qquad$ $\dfrac{4}{5} \div \dfrac{2}{7}$ $\qquad$ $\dfrac{7}{4} \div \dfrac{8}{5}$

$$\frac{9}{7} \div \frac{7}{6} \qquad \frac{7}{3} \div \frac{2}{9} \qquad \frac{5}{2} \div \frac{2}{9} \qquad \frac{4}{3} \div \frac{5}{8} \qquad \frac{9}{5} \div \frac{1}{4}$$

$$\frac{3}{5} \div \frac{5}{9} \qquad \frac{8}{9} \div \frac{1}{8} \qquad \frac{1}{7} \div \frac{9}{8} \qquad \frac{1}{4} \div \frac{9}{2} \qquad \frac{5}{4} \div \frac{4}{7}$$

$$\frac{5}{9} \div \frac{3}{5} \qquad \frac{3}{8} \div \frac{9}{8} \qquad \frac{5}{3} \div \frac{4}{5} \qquad \frac{3}{7} \div \frac{3}{5} \qquad \frac{9}{4} \div \frac{4}{7}$$

$$\frac{1}{7} \div \frac{2}{7} \qquad \frac{5}{4} \div \frac{8}{7} \qquad \frac{6}{7} \div \frac{5}{9} \qquad \frac{7}{6} \div \frac{2}{3} \qquad \frac{1}{2} \div \frac{9}{8}$$

$$\frac{1}{5} \div \frac{9}{2} \qquad \frac{3}{7} \div \frac{8}{3} \qquad \frac{5}{2} \div \frac{8}{3} \qquad \frac{4}{7} \div \frac{7}{6} \qquad \frac{2}{7} \div \frac{8}{9}$$

$\dfrac{2}{5} \div \dfrac{3}{8}$ $\qquad$ $\dfrac{2}{7} \div \dfrac{5}{4}$ $\qquad$ $\dfrac{1}{5} \div \dfrac{7}{9}$ $\qquad$ $\dfrac{7}{6} \div \dfrac{1}{8}$ $\qquad$ $\dfrac{2}{5} \div \dfrac{2}{7}$

$\dfrac{9}{4} \div \dfrac{1}{9}$ $\qquad$ $\dfrac{1}{6} \div \dfrac{7}{5}$ $\qquad$ $\dfrac{8}{5} \div \dfrac{2}{9}$ $\qquad$ $\dfrac{4}{7} \div \dfrac{8}{3}$ $\qquad$ $\dfrac{3}{4} \div \dfrac{4}{3}$

$\dfrac{2}{5} \div \dfrac{1}{8}$ $\qquad$ $\dfrac{5}{8} \div \dfrac{1}{3}$ $\qquad$ $\dfrac{5}{4} \div \dfrac{3}{2}$ $\qquad$ $\dfrac{3}{7} \div \dfrac{6}{5}$ $\qquad$ $\dfrac{9}{8} \div \dfrac{4}{3}$

$\dfrac{9}{5} \div \dfrac{7}{8}$ $\qquad$ $\dfrac{5}{7} \div \dfrac{3}{8}$ $\qquad$ $\dfrac{7}{4} \div \dfrac{1}{2}$ $\qquad$ $\dfrac{1}{7} \div \dfrac{9}{5}$ $\qquad$ $\dfrac{2}{3} \div \dfrac{2}{7}$

$\dfrac{3}{8} \div \dfrac{8}{7}$ $\qquad$ $\dfrac{2}{7} \div \dfrac{1}{8}$ $\qquad$ $\dfrac{7}{8} \div \dfrac{1}{5}$ $\qquad$ $\dfrac{7}{6} \div \dfrac{5}{7}$ $\qquad$ $\dfrac{8}{7} \div \dfrac{1}{4}$

$\frac{7}{4} \div \frac{5}{6}$ $\frac{4}{5} \div \frac{2}{7}$ $\frac{7}{5} \div \frac{9}{7}$ $\frac{1}{9} \div \frac{8}{5}$ $\frac{7}{8} \div \frac{1}{2}$

$\frac{7}{3} \div \frac{1}{4}$ $\frac{3}{8} \div \frac{9}{8}$ $\frac{2}{9} \div \frac{5}{3}$ $\frac{8}{7} \div \frac{7}{6}$ $\frac{8}{7} \div \frac{8}{5}$

$\frac{1}{4} \div \frac{7}{9}$ $\frac{4}{7} \div \frac{5}{9}$ $\frac{2}{9} \div \frac{1}{7}$ $\frac{5}{6} \div \frac{5}{3}$ $\frac{5}{3} \div \frac{6}{7}$

$\frac{1}{6} \div \frac{4}{7}$ $\frac{3}{2} \div \frac{5}{6}$ $\frac{8}{9} \div \frac{1}{6}$ $\frac{5}{8} \div \frac{7}{8}$ $\frac{1}{8} \div \frac{7}{9}$

$\frac{3}{5} \div \frac{4}{3}$ $\frac{9}{8} \div \frac{5}{9}$ $\frac{3}{7} \div \frac{4}{5}$ $\frac{3}{8} \div \frac{7}{8}$ $\frac{9}{8} \div \frac{6}{5}$

$$\frac{7}{2} \div \frac{5}{2} \qquad \frac{3}{8} \div \frac{9}{7} \qquad \frac{9}{8} \div \frac{2}{3} \qquad \frac{2}{3} \div \frac{3}{8} \qquad \frac{4}{3} \div \frac{7}{2}$$

$$\frac{7}{5} \div \frac{3}{4} \qquad \frac{8}{3} \div \frac{5}{7} \qquad \frac{2}{7} \div \frac{9}{2} \qquad \frac{2}{3} \div \frac{5}{4} \qquad \frac{7}{4} \div \frac{7}{5}$$

$$\frac{7}{4} \div \frac{7}{3} \qquad \frac{1}{7} \div \frac{8}{7} \qquad \frac{5}{2} \div \frac{9}{5} \qquad \frac{8}{3} \div \frac{3}{4} \qquad \frac{1}{4} \div \frac{7}{5}$$

$$\frac{7}{4} \div \frac{3}{7} \qquad \frac{4}{3} \div \frac{3}{5} \qquad \frac{1}{5} \div \frac{8}{5} \qquad \frac{4}{7} \div \frac{9}{5} \qquad \frac{2}{5} \div \frac{4}{3}$$

$$\frac{7}{6} \div \frac{2}{5} \qquad \frac{1}{3} \div \frac{2}{3} \qquad \frac{1}{7} \div \frac{3}{5} \qquad \frac{3}{2} \div \frac{8}{5} \qquad \frac{5}{7} \div \frac{6}{5}$$

$\dfrac{1}{2} \div \dfrac{5}{2}$ $\dfrac{5}{8} \div \dfrac{1}{7}$ $\dfrac{4}{7} \div \dfrac{3}{8}$ $\dfrac{5}{7} \div \dfrac{1}{6}$ $\dfrac{7}{8} \div \dfrac{1}{4}$

$\dfrac{2}{3} \div \dfrac{7}{8}$ $\dfrac{3}{4} \div \dfrac{6}{5}$ $\dfrac{7}{8} \div \dfrac{4}{5}$ $\dfrac{3}{5} \div \dfrac{5}{4}$ $\dfrac{1}{9} \div \dfrac{7}{4}$

$\dfrac{6}{5} \div \dfrac{7}{6}$ $\dfrac{8}{3} \div \dfrac{5}{4}$ $\dfrac{9}{5} \div \dfrac{9}{2}$ $\dfrac{5}{4} \div \dfrac{9}{8}$ $\dfrac{5}{8} \div \dfrac{7}{6}$

$\dfrac{1}{9} \div \dfrac{1}{3}$ $\dfrac{1}{4} \div \dfrac{1}{6}$ $\dfrac{5}{6} \div \dfrac{5}{9}$ $\dfrac{7}{9} \div \dfrac{1}{4}$ $\dfrac{6}{7} \div \dfrac{1}{6}$

$\dfrac{6}{5} \div \dfrac{2}{7}$ $\dfrac{2}{7} \div \dfrac{6}{7}$ $\dfrac{6}{5} \div \dfrac{8}{7}$ $\dfrac{8}{3} \div \dfrac{9}{2}$ $\dfrac{9}{2} \div \dfrac{5}{8}$

$$\frac{1}{7} \div \frac{8}{3} \qquad \frac{5}{6} \div \frac{3}{4} \qquad \frac{4}{9} \div \frac{4}{3} \qquad \frac{4}{5} \div \frac{3}{2} \qquad \frac{1}{6} \div \frac{9}{5}$$

$$\frac{7}{2} \div \frac{9}{7} \qquad \frac{1}{3} \div \frac{5}{7} \qquad \frac{4}{9} \div \frac{4}{3} \qquad \frac{9}{7} \div \frac{7}{2} \qquad \frac{3}{8} \div \frac{2}{5}$$

$$\frac{5}{4} \div \frac{7}{8} \qquad \frac{1}{7} \div \frac{4}{5} \qquad \frac{8}{9} \div \frac{3}{7} \qquad \frac{5}{4} \div \frac{4}{3} \qquad \frac{1}{9} \div \frac{4}{9}$$

$$\frac{7}{6} \div \frac{4}{9} \qquad \frac{2}{5} \div \frac{8}{5} \qquad \frac{3}{2} \div \frac{1}{9} \qquad \frac{6}{5} \div \frac{3}{7} \qquad \frac{1}{7} \div \frac{6}{5}$$

$$\frac{1}{8} \div \frac{4}{9} \qquad \frac{5}{4} \div \frac{1}{7} \qquad \frac{5}{3} \div \frac{5}{7} \qquad \frac{9}{7} \div \frac{8}{9} \qquad \frac{3}{7} \div \frac{5}{3}$$

$\frac{5}{6} \div \frac{3}{5}$ $\frac{6}{5} \div \frac{3}{8}$ $\frac{8}{5} \div \frac{2}{7}$ $\frac{5}{7} \div \frac{5}{8}$ $\frac{1}{6} \div \frac{9}{5}$

$\frac{3}{5} \div \frac{8}{5}$ $\frac{7}{9} \div \frac{2}{9}$ $\frac{1}{5} \div \frac{3}{5}$ $\frac{8}{9} \div \frac{5}{2}$ $\frac{1}{5} \div \frac{7}{4}$

$\frac{9}{8} \div \frac{7}{2}$ $\frac{3}{2} \div \frac{8}{3}$ $\frac{8}{3} \div \frac{9}{7}$ $\frac{9}{8} \div \frac{5}{8}$ $\frac{5}{2} \div \frac{9}{5}$

$\frac{7}{5} \div \frac{1}{2}$ $\frac{9}{2} \div \frac{7}{9}$ $\frac{6}{7} \div \frac{3}{2}$ $\frac{1}{6} \div \frac{3}{5}$ $\frac{5}{9} \div \frac{8}{3}$

$\frac{1}{7} \div \frac{1}{4}$ $\frac{7}{4} \div \frac{9}{4}$ $\frac{5}{4} \div \frac{5}{7}$ $\frac{8}{9} \div \frac{1}{8}$ $\frac{8}{7} \div \frac{3}{2}$

$\dfrac{7}{3} \div \dfrac{6}{5}$ $\dfrac{1}{5} \div \dfrac{3}{4}$ $\dfrac{7}{8} \div \dfrac{5}{9}$ $\dfrac{4}{3} \div \dfrac{1}{7}$ $\dfrac{1}{6} \div \dfrac{3}{8}$

$\dfrac{6}{7} \div \dfrac{7}{6}$ $\dfrac{3}{4} \div \dfrac{5}{8}$ $\dfrac{8}{7} \div \dfrac{3}{2}$ $\dfrac{1}{3} \div \dfrac{3}{4}$ $\dfrac{1}{9} \div \dfrac{2}{9}$

$\dfrac{5}{9} \div \dfrac{1}{3}$ $\dfrac{1}{2} \div \dfrac{3}{8}$ $\dfrac{3}{7} \div \dfrac{1}{3}$ $\dfrac{2}{7} \div \dfrac{1}{8}$ $\dfrac{7}{9} \div \dfrac{5}{2}$

$\dfrac{9}{7} \div \dfrac{6}{5}$ $\dfrac{7}{5} \div \dfrac{1}{4}$ $\dfrac{5}{9} \div \dfrac{8}{9}$ $\dfrac{9}{5} \div \dfrac{3}{4}$ $\dfrac{7}{4} \div \dfrac{4}{7}$

$\dfrac{7}{4} \div \dfrac{5}{6}$ $\dfrac{2}{9} \div \dfrac{6}{5}$ $\dfrac{4}{9} \div \dfrac{4}{3}$ $\dfrac{2}{5} \div \dfrac{7}{5}$ $\dfrac{6}{5} \div \dfrac{1}{4}$

$\dfrac{2}{7} \div \dfrac{1}{5}$ $\dfrac{4}{3} \div \dfrac{5}{7}$ $\dfrac{3}{8} \div \dfrac{2}{5}$ $\dfrac{6}{7} \div \dfrac{7}{9}$ $\dfrac{1}{8} \div \dfrac{9}{2}$

$\dfrac{2}{9} \div \dfrac{3}{5}$ $\dfrac{1}{4} \div \dfrac{4}{7}$ $\dfrac{9}{2} \div \dfrac{7}{8}$ $\dfrac{8}{7} \div \dfrac{5}{7}$ $\dfrac{8}{9} \div \dfrac{2}{3}$

$\dfrac{4}{5} \div \dfrac{4}{3}$ $\dfrac{1}{2} \div \dfrac{2}{9}$ $\dfrac{2}{3} \div \dfrac{8}{3}$ $\dfrac{1}{6} \div \dfrac{5}{3}$ $\dfrac{5}{3} \div \dfrac{9}{2}$

$\dfrac{1}{2} \div \dfrac{9}{4}$ $\dfrac{9}{5} \div \dfrac{5}{4}$ $\dfrac{8}{7} \div \dfrac{3}{5}$ $\dfrac{2}{9} \div \dfrac{8}{5}$ $\dfrac{1}{5} \div \dfrac{1}{4}$

$\dfrac{4}{5} \div \dfrac{9}{7}$ $\dfrac{3}{4} \div \dfrac{8}{3}$ $\dfrac{7}{6} \div \dfrac{9}{5}$ $\dfrac{5}{6} \div \dfrac{7}{5}$ $\dfrac{3}{4} \div \dfrac{1}{7}$

Answer Key

Part 1 Answers:

Page 7

$\frac{13}{10}$ $\frac{47}{12}$ $\frac{31}{21}$ $\frac{13}{21}$ $\frac{31}{42}$

$\frac{61}{42}$ $\frac{11}{9}$ $\frac{13}{8}$ $\frac{5}{2}$ $\frac{13}{42}$

$\frac{31}{10}$ $\frac{9}{5}$ $\frac{45}{56}$ $\frac{29}{6}$ $\frac{77}{24}$

$\frac{12}{7}$ $\frac{12}{7}$ $\frac{19}{4}$ $\frac{35}{18}$ $\frac{14}{9}$

$\frac{25}{36}$ $\frac{59}{12}$ $\frac{67}{56}$ $\frac{93}{35}$ $\frac{79}{24}$

Page 8

$\frac{22}{9}$ $\frac{53}{56}$ $\frac{39}{28}$ $\frac{22}{15}$ $\frac{79}{40}$

$\frac{37}{24}$ $\frac{13}{15}$ $\frac{15}{4}$ $\frac{17}{20}$ $\frac{19}{8}$

$\frac{19}{6}$ $\frac{97}{72}$ $\frac{49}{24}$ $\frac{33}{20}$ $\frac{9}{4}$

$\frac{16}{3}$ $\frac{35}{6}$ $\frac{17}{8}$ $\frac{3}{4}$ $\frac{7}{5}$

$\frac{71}{40}$ $\frac{89}{36}$ $\frac{8}{9}$ $\frac{53}{20}$ $\frac{58}{63}$

Page 9

$\frac{95}{28}$ $\frac{37}{35}$ $\frac{74}{21}$ $\frac{62}{45}$ $\frac{9}{7}$

$\frac{61}{42}$ $\frac{35}{12}$ $\frac{12}{35}$ $\frac{17}{35}$ $\frac{17}{12}$

$\frac{12}{5}$ $\frac{81}{28}$ $\frac{61}{28}$ $\frac{80}{21}$ $\frac{11}{15}$

$\frac{46}{35}$ $\frac{7}{3}$ $\frac{1}{2}$ $\frac{13}{8}$ $\frac{31}{18}$

$\frac{11}{14}$ $\frac{110}{63}$ $\frac{7}{9}$ $\frac{37}{18}$ $\frac{25}{9}$

Page 10

$\frac{37}{18}$ $\frac{113}{56}$ $\frac{65}{24}$ $\frac{47}{42}$ $\frac{75}{28}$

$\frac{108}{35}$ $\frac{7}{9}$ $\frac{25}{18}$ $\frac{47}{30}$ $\frac{47}{14}$

$\frac{95}{28}$ $\frac{46}{21}$ $\frac{37}{35}$ $\frac{5}{12}$ $\frac{21}{40}$

$\frac{17}{24}$ $\frac{25}{12}$ $\frac{92}{45}$ $\frac{13}{8}$ $\frac{27}{20}$

$\frac{71}{18}$ $\frac{15}{4}$ $\frac{55}{36}$ $\frac{43}{6}$ $\frac{31}{6}$

Page 11

$\frac{5}{8}$ $\frac{32}{15}$ $\frac{55}{12}$ $\frac{101}{40}$ $\frac{27}{4}$

$\frac{97}{72}$ $\frac{25}{6}$ $\frac{97}{56}$ $\frac{26}{9}$ $\frac{52}{21}$

$\frac{19}{6}$ $\frac{49}{20}$ $\frac{28}{15}$ $\frac{29}{6}$ $\frac{37}{14}$

$\frac{145}{72}$ $\frac{31}{18}$ $\frac{67}{28}$ $\frac{31}{10}$ $\frac{21}{40}$

$\frac{59}{35}$ $\frac{16}{5}$ $\frac{87}{28}$ $\frac{49}{36}$ $\frac{17}{6}$

Page 12

$\frac{13}{20}$ $\frac{19}{24}$ $\frac{54}{35}$ $\frac{101}{40}$ $\frac{87}{35}$

$\frac{56}{15}$ $\frac{128}{63}$ $\frac{23}{12}$ $\frac{85}{18}$ $\frac{34}{21}$

$\frac{89}{42}$ $\frac{5}{3}$ $\frac{14}{5}$ $\frac{51}{14}$ $\frac{5}{12}$

$\frac{15}{4}$ $\frac{13}{12}$ $\frac{35}{24}$ $\frac{23}{40}$ $\frac{9}{8}$

$\frac{49}{20}$ $\frac{35}{24}$ $\frac{3}{2}$ $\frac{9}{7}$ $\frac{23}{15}$

Page 13

$\frac{39}{40}$ $\frac{73}{14}$ $\frac{21}{10}$ $\frac{44}{15}$ $\frac{79}{24}$

$\frac{17}{15}$ $\frac{65}{36}$ $\frac{41}{24}$ $\frac{57}{28}$ $\frac{11}{6}$

$\frac{9}{7}$ $\frac{10}{9}$ $\frac{41}{18}$ $\frac{101}{63}$ $\frac{34}{35}$

$\frac{27}{4}$ $\frac{81}{20}$ $\frac{61}{40}$ $\frac{11}{9}$ $\frac{73}{21}$

$\frac{51}{40}$ $\frac{67}{72}$ $\frac{21}{8}$ $\frac{82}{63}$ $\frac{53}{28}$

Page 14

$\frac{45}{8}$ $\frac{37}{6}$ $\frac{79}{45}$ $\frac{9}{20}$ $\frac{128}{63}$

$\frac{31}{18}$ $\frac{13}{14}$ $\frac{9}{10}$ $\frac{79}{42}$ $\frac{91}{36}$

$\frac{29}{18}$ $\frac{51}{20}$ $\frac{41}{30}$ $\frac{43}{8}$ $\frac{53}{14}$

$\frac{116}{63}$ $\frac{67}{20}$ $\frac{4}{3}$ $\frac{31}{20}$ $\frac{13}{8}$

$\frac{17}{7}$ $\frac{7}{3}$ $\frac{64}{35}$ $\frac{59}{72}$ $\frac{31}{10}$

Page 15

$\dfrac{11}{5}$ $\qquad$ $\dfrac{7}{9}$ $\qquad$ $\dfrac{43}{12}$ $\qquad$ $\dfrac{83}{45}$ $\qquad$ $\dfrac{4}{5}$

$\dfrac{14}{9}$ $\qquad$ $\dfrac{39}{28}$ $\qquad$ $\dfrac{25}{14}$ $\qquad$ $\dfrac{57}{35}$ $\qquad$ $\dfrac{64}{45}$

$\dfrac{86}{63}$ $\qquad$ $\dfrac{37}{8}$ $\qquad$ $\dfrac{58}{21}$ $\qquad$ $\dfrac{62}{21}$ $\qquad$ $\dfrac{11}{6}$

$\dfrac{29}{9}$ $\qquad$ $\dfrac{53}{15}$ $\qquad$ $\dfrac{77}{18}$ $\qquad$ $\dfrac{109}{36}$ $\qquad$ $\dfrac{23}{12}$

$\dfrac{66}{35}$ $\qquad$ $\dfrac{9}{20}$ $\qquad$ $\dfrac{87}{35}$ $\qquad$ $\dfrac{5}{7}$ $\qquad$ $\dfrac{49}{36}$

Page 16

$\dfrac{73}{18}$ $\qquad$ $\dfrac{89}{18}$ $\qquad$ $\dfrac{77}{45}$ $\qquad$ $\dfrac{7}{8}$ $\qquad$ $\dfrac{71}{45}$

$\dfrac{2}{3}$ $\qquad$ $\dfrac{39}{20}$ $\qquad$ $\dfrac{32}{15}$ $\qquad$ $\dfrac{87}{35}$ $\qquad$ $\dfrac{23}{6}$

$\dfrac{23}{4}$ $\qquad$ $\dfrac{61}{56}$ $\qquad$ $\dfrac{61}{63}$ $\qquad$ $\dfrac{23}{4}$ $\qquad$ $\dfrac{17}{8}$

$\dfrac{49}{20}$ $\qquad$ $\dfrac{65}{56}$ $\qquad$ $\dfrac{107}{40}$ $\qquad$ $\dfrac{33}{28}$ $\qquad$ $\dfrac{46}{21}$

$\dfrac{71}{28}$ $\qquad$ $\dfrac{15}{7}$ $\qquad$ $\dfrac{77}{40}$ $\qquad$ $\dfrac{25}{72}$ $\qquad$ $\dfrac{3}{7}$

Page 17

$\dfrac{77}{36}$ $\qquad$ $\dfrac{57}{56}$ $\qquad$ $\dfrac{21}{4}$ $\qquad$ $\dfrac{81}{40}$ $\qquad$ $\dfrac{57}{40}$

$\dfrac{71}{36}$ $\qquad$ $\dfrac{43}{20}$ $\qquad$ $\dfrac{47}{10}$ $\qquad$ $\dfrac{43}{63}$ $\qquad$ $\dfrac{5}{2}$

$\dfrac{25}{12}$ $\qquad$ $\dfrac{29}{6}$ $\qquad$ $\dfrac{6}{5}$ $\qquad$ $\dfrac{71}{42}$ $\qquad$ $\dfrac{11}{9}$

$\dfrac{24}{35}$ $\qquad$ $\dfrac{67}{21}$ $\qquad$ $\dfrac{15}{8}$ $\qquad$ $\dfrac{7}{4}$ $\qquad$ $\dfrac{17}{18}$

$\dfrac{5}{3}$ $\qquad$ $\dfrac{11}{30}$ $\qquad$ $\dfrac{12}{35}$ $\qquad$ $\dfrac{19}{24}$ $\qquad$ $\dfrac{46}{21}$

Page 18

$\dfrac{7}{24}$ $\qquad$ $\dfrac{9}{4}$ $\qquad$ $\dfrac{17}{5}$ $\qquad$ $\dfrac{9}{14}$ $\qquad$ $\dfrac{29}{12}$

$\dfrac{8}{15}$ $\qquad$ $\dfrac{100}{63}$ $\qquad$ $\dfrac{53}{30}$ $\qquad$ $\dfrac{29}{20}$ $\qquad$ $\dfrac{35}{24}$

$\dfrac{103}{45}$ $\qquad$ $\dfrac{1}{2}$ $\qquad$ $\dfrac{65}{18}$ $\qquad$ $\dfrac{17}{6}$ $\qquad$ $\dfrac{79}{40}$

$\dfrac{19}{35}$ $\qquad$ $\dfrac{5}{3}$ $\qquad$ $\dfrac{78}{35}$ $\qquad$ $\dfrac{25}{9}$ $\qquad$ $\dfrac{67}{24}$

$\dfrac{59}{72}$ $\qquad$ $\dfrac{72}{35}$ $\qquad$ $\dfrac{35}{6}$ $\qquad$ $\dfrac{83}{24}$ $\qquad$ $\dfrac{95}{28}$

Page 19

$\dfrac{71}{45}$ $\qquad$ $\dfrac{5}{3}$ $\qquad$ $\dfrac{4}{9}$ $\qquad$ $\dfrac{79}{42}$ $\qquad$ $\dfrac{61}{45}$

$\dfrac{9}{10}$ $\qquad$ $\dfrac{107}{63}$ $\qquad$ $\dfrac{29}{18}$ $\qquad$ $\dfrac{17}{6}$ $\qquad$ $\dfrac{65}{24}$

$\dfrac{4}{5}$ $\qquad$ $\dfrac{97}{56}$ $\qquad$ $\dfrac{107}{56}$ $\qquad$ $\dfrac{35}{18}$ $\qquad$ $\dfrac{29}{35}$

$\dfrac{96}{35}$ $\qquad$ $\dfrac{95}{28}$ $\qquad$ $\dfrac{47}{18}$ $\qquad$ $\dfrac{21}{8}$ $\qquad$ $\dfrac{49}{10}$

$\dfrac{9}{4}$ $\qquad$ $\dfrac{40}{21}$ $\qquad$ $\dfrac{19}{35}$ $\qquad$ $\dfrac{13}{4}$ $\qquad$ $\dfrac{92}{45}$

Page 20

$\dfrac{7}{18}$ $\qquad$ $\dfrac{23}{14}$ $\qquad$ $\dfrac{21}{20}$ $\qquad$ $\dfrac{73}{35}$ $\qquad$ $\dfrac{33}{8}$

$\dfrac{25}{42}$ $\qquad$ $\dfrac{86}{63}$ $\qquad$ $\dfrac{55}{14}$ $\qquad$ $\dfrac{59}{56}$ $\qquad$ $\dfrac{39}{14}$

$\dfrac{41}{21}$ $\qquad$ $\dfrac{32}{21}$ $\qquad$ $\dfrac{31}{10}$ $\qquad$ $\dfrac{41}{10}$ $\qquad$ $\dfrac{59}{35}$

$\dfrac{39}{10}$ $\qquad$ $\dfrac{77}{40}$ $\qquad$ $\dfrac{41}{24}$ $\qquad$ $\dfrac{55}{63}$ $\qquad$ $\dfrac{9}{5}$

$\dfrac{29}{45}$ $\qquad$ $\dfrac{85}{36}$ $\qquad$ $\dfrac{47}{21}$ $\qquad$ $\dfrac{121}{63}$ $\qquad$ $\dfrac{79}{18}$

Page 21

$\dfrac{97}{42}$ $\qquad$ $\dfrac{53}{10}$ $\qquad$ $\dfrac{17}{6}$ $\qquad$ $\dfrac{17}{18}$ $\qquad$ $\dfrac{11}{6}$

$\dfrac{25}{18}$ $\qquad$ $\dfrac{35}{12}$ $\qquad$ $\dfrac{35}{18}$ $\qquad$ $\dfrac{43}{12}$ $\qquad$ $\dfrac{29}{21}$

$\dfrac{11}{6}$ $\qquad$ $\dfrac{83}{28}$ $\qquad$ $\dfrac{11}{8}$ $\qquad$ $\dfrac{34}{21}$ $\qquad$ $\dfrac{61}{20}$

$\dfrac{19}{6}$ $\qquad$ $\dfrac{53}{14}$ $\qquad$ $\dfrac{35}{24}$ $\qquad$ $\dfrac{5}{2}$ $\qquad$ $\dfrac{9}{8}$

$\dfrac{13}{3}$ $\qquad$ $\dfrac{31}{18}$ $\qquad$ $\dfrac{27}{28}$ $\qquad$ $\dfrac{87}{56}$ $\qquad$ $\dfrac{17}{10}$

Page 22

$\dfrac{61}{20}$ $\qquad$ $\dfrac{65}{42}$ $\qquad$ $\dfrac{31}{8}$ $\qquad$ $\dfrac{27}{14}$ $\qquad$ $\dfrac{61}{24}$

$\dfrac{55}{56}$ $\qquad$ $\dfrac{68}{21}$ $\qquad$ $\dfrac{55}{14}$ $\qquad$ $\dfrac{69}{28}$ $\qquad$ $\dfrac{11}{24}$

$\dfrac{17}{72}$ $\qquad$ $\dfrac{25}{24}$ $\qquad$ $\dfrac{71}{40}$ $\qquad$ $\dfrac{59}{42}$ $\qquad$ $\dfrac{17}{14}$

$\dfrac{101}{72}$ $\qquad$ $\dfrac{76}{35}$ $\qquad$ $\dfrac{83}{18}$ $\qquad$ $\dfrac{23}{63}$ $\qquad$ $\dfrac{103}{45}$

$\dfrac{14}{5}$ $\qquad$ $\dfrac{69}{40}$ $\qquad$ $\dfrac{94}{63}$ $\qquad$ $\dfrac{37}{10}$ $\qquad$ $\dfrac{19}{15}$

Page   23

$\dfrac{121}{56}$	$\dfrac{55}{36}$	$\dfrac{89}{42}$	$\dfrac{12}{5}$	$\dfrac{31}{12}$
$\dfrac{27}{8}$	$\dfrac{13}{4}$	$\dfrac{11}{7}$	$\dfrac{61}{36}$	$\dfrac{10}{9}$
$\dfrac{11}{14}$	$\dfrac{39}{20}$	$\dfrac{13}{15}$	$\dfrac{3}{4}$	$\dfrac{51}{40}$
$\dfrac{23}{9}$	$\dfrac{101}{35}$	$\dfrac{13}{10}$	$\dfrac{22}{35}$	$\dfrac{45}{56}$
$\dfrac{88}{35}$	$\dfrac{8}{3}$	$\dfrac{43}{15}$	$\dfrac{39}{40}$	$\dfrac{65}{36}$

Page   24

$\dfrac{95}{56}$	$\dfrac{59}{45}$	$\dfrac{67}{35}$	$\dfrac{67}{24}$	$\dfrac{19}{15}$
$\dfrac{44}{21}$	$\dfrac{79}{56}$	$\dfrac{73}{30}$	$\dfrac{55}{14}$	$\dfrac{103}{72}$
$\dfrac{33}{14}$	$\dfrac{86}{45}$	$\dfrac{61}{10}$	$\dfrac{79}{45}$	$\dfrac{29}{56}$
$\dfrac{34}{15}$	$\dfrac{17}{6}$	$\dfrac{19}{15}$	$\dfrac{41}{20}$	$\dfrac{17}{20}$
$\dfrac{87}{56}$	$\dfrac{5}{2}$	$\dfrac{47}{30}$	$\dfrac{107}{56}$	$\dfrac{99}{56}$

Page   25

$\dfrac{65}{72}$	$\dfrac{17}{15}$	$\dfrac{29}{14}$	$\dfrac{11}{5}$	$\dfrac{47}{24}$
$\dfrac{71}{28}$	$\dfrac{46}{15}$	$\dfrac{95}{18}$	$\dfrac{37}{14}$	$\dfrac{13}{18}$
$\dfrac{67}{45}$	$\dfrac{29}{56}$	$\dfrac{35}{24}$	$\dfrac{93}{56}$	$\dfrac{51}{10}$
$\dfrac{25}{63}$	$\dfrac{61}{40}$	$\dfrac{57}{28}$	$\dfrac{11}{6}$	$\dfrac{11}{24}$
$\dfrac{44}{15}$	$\dfrac{31}{24}$	$\dfrac{25}{24}$	$\dfrac{34}{21}$	$\dfrac{11}{7}$

Page   26

$\dfrac{81}{14}$	$\dfrac{57}{20}$	$\dfrac{39}{28}$	$\dfrac{59}{20}$	$\dfrac{59}{42}$
$\dfrac{41}{12}$	$\dfrac{19}{12}$	$\dfrac{59}{42}$	$\dfrac{2}{3}$	$\dfrac{14}{5}$
$\dfrac{19}{45}$	$\dfrac{23}{63}$	$\dfrac{7}{5}$	$\dfrac{9}{14}$	$\dfrac{17}{14}$
$\dfrac{87}{40}$	$\dfrac{35}{8}$	$\dfrac{79}{35}$	$\dfrac{17}{5}$	$\dfrac{11}{6}$
$\dfrac{4}{7}$	$\dfrac{68}{45}$	$\dfrac{81}{40}$	$\dfrac{43}{28}$	$\dfrac{31}{36}$

Page   27

$\dfrac{5}{8}$	$\dfrac{107}{40}$	$\dfrac{37}{35}$	$\dfrac{31}{6}$	$\dfrac{19}{12}$
$\dfrac{9}{4}$	$\dfrac{33}{20}$	$\dfrac{110}{63}$	$\dfrac{24}{35}$	$\dfrac{49}{36}$
$\dfrac{11}{12}$	$\dfrac{83}{21}$	$\dfrac{31}{28}$	$\dfrac{43}{24}$	$\dfrac{97}{45}$
$\dfrac{25}{42}$	$\dfrac{53}{72}$	$\dfrac{25}{24}$	$\dfrac{101}{40}$	$\dfrac{51}{35}$
$\dfrac{59}{10}$	$\dfrac{35}{12}$	$\dfrac{95}{56}$	$\dfrac{17}{12}$	$\dfrac{13}{5}$

Page   28

$\dfrac{121}{45}$	$\dfrac{23}{30}$	$\dfrac{29}{8}$	$\dfrac{19}{8}$	$\dfrac{73}{24}$
$\dfrac{16}{5}$	$\dfrac{29}{12}$	$\dfrac{38}{15}$	$\dfrac{25}{36}$	$\dfrac{25}{42}$
$\dfrac{80}{63}$	$\dfrac{9}{20}$	$\dfrac{31}{28}$	$\dfrac{28}{45}$	$\dfrac{21}{8}$
$\dfrac{67}{18}$	$\dfrac{67}{14}$	$\dfrac{113}{36}$	$\dfrac{66}{35}$	$\dfrac{9}{5}$
$\dfrac{43}{36}$	$\dfrac{47}{10}$	$\dfrac{43}{35}$	$\dfrac{23}{12}$	$\dfrac{88}{35}$

Page   29

$\dfrac{32}{15}$	$\dfrac{16}{7}$	$\dfrac{25}{6}$	$\dfrac{49}{18}$	$\dfrac{61}{45}$
$\dfrac{56}{45}$	$\dfrac{109}{72}$	$\dfrac{22}{35}$	$\dfrac{47}{15}$	$\dfrac{101}{40}$
$\dfrac{7}{4}$	$\dfrac{38}{35}$	$\dfrac{39}{35}$	$\dfrac{13}{5}$	$\dfrac{11}{9}$
$\dfrac{73}{20}$	$\dfrac{61}{45}$	$\dfrac{27}{20}$	$\dfrac{17}{18}$	$\dfrac{75}{14}$
$\dfrac{11}{9}$	$\dfrac{73}{28}$	$\dfrac{23}{20}$	$\dfrac{44}{21}$	$\dfrac{55}{24}$

Page   30

$\dfrac{55}{14}$	$\dfrac{64}{63}$	$\dfrac{47}{36}$	$\dfrac{85}{72}$	$\dfrac{71}{20}$
$\dfrac{53}{10}$	$\dfrac{27}{28}$	$\dfrac{31}{15}$	$\dfrac{81}{14}$	$\dfrac{16}{9}$
$\dfrac{74}{21}$	$\dfrac{83}{45}$	$\dfrac{80}{21}$	$\dfrac{14}{45}$	$\dfrac{17}{6}$
$\dfrac{107}{40}$	$\dfrac{59}{12}$	$\dfrac{5}{2}$	$\dfrac{7}{10}$	$\dfrac{29}{12}$
$\dfrac{11}{6}$	$\dfrac{7}{8}$	$\dfrac{5}{3}$	$\dfrac{61}{30}$	$\dfrac{53}{40}$

Page 31

$\frac{17}{6}$	$\frac{9}{7}$	$\frac{71}{63}$	$\frac{35}{8}$	$\frac{65}{42}$
$\frac{58}{21}$	$\frac{112}{45}$	$\frac{19}{6}$	$\frac{18}{5}$	$\frac{65}{72}$
$\frac{62}{35}$	$\frac{8}{7}$	$\frac{47}{40}$	$\frac{17}{6}$	$\frac{79}{72}$
$\frac{11}{12}$	$\frac{95}{28}$	$\frac{41}{21}$	$\frac{53}{63}$	$\frac{12}{35}$
$\frac{13}{8}$	$\frac{41}{72}$	$\frac{87}{40}$	$\frac{58}{35}$	$\frac{57}{56}$

Part 2 Answers:

Page 33

$\frac{1}{21}$	$\frac{13}{24}$	$\frac{17}{40}$	$\frac{7}{30}$	$\frac{7}{24}$
$\frac{2}{63}$	$\frac{29}{21}$	$\frac{1}{6}$	$\frac{32}{45}$	$\frac{22}{45}$
$\frac{23}{9}$	$\frac{8}{15}$	$\frac{1}{6}$	$\frac{27}{56}$	$\frac{1}{45}$
$\frac{49}{36}$	$\frac{1}{5}$	$\frac{7}{6}$	$\frac{61}{36}$	$\frac{2}{9}$
$\frac{6}{5}$	$\frac{29}{30}$	$\frac{77}{18}$	$\frac{3}{5}$	$\frac{13}{40}$

Page 34

$\frac{27}{56}$	$\frac{7}{40}$	$\frac{2}{9}$	$\frac{19}{8}$	$\frac{19}{6}$
$\frac{10}{63}$	$\frac{43}{40}$	$\frac{3}{4}$	$\frac{17}{24}$	$\frac{17}{30}$
$\frac{5}{6}$	$\frac{13}{12}$	$\frac{20}{63}$	$\frac{1}{56}$	$\frac{5}{72}$
$\frac{1}{7}$	$\frac{1}{42}$	$\frac{31}{30}$	$\frac{1}{4}$	$\frac{5}{4}$
$\frac{1}{7}$	$\frac{19}{21}$	$\frac{13}{8}$	$\frac{26}{15}$	$\frac{7}{3}$

Page 35

$\frac{2}{21}$	$\frac{1}{20}$	$\frac{27}{40}$	$\frac{28}{15}$	$\frac{5}{56}$
$\frac{3}{10}$	$\frac{1}{72}$	$\frac{29}{40}$	$\frac{31}{21}$	$\frac{1}{8}$
$\frac{19}{12}$	$\frac{23}{9}$	$\frac{11}{15}$	$\frac{13}{10}$	$\frac{27}{20}$
$\frac{16}{15}$	$\frac{1}{4}$	$\frac{9}{10}$	$\frac{17}{9}$	$\frac{31}{10}$
$\frac{2}{5}$	$\frac{11}{6}$	$\frac{2}{63}$	$\frac{1}{3}$	$\frac{4}{3}$

Page 36

$\frac{2}{21}$	$\frac{4}{5}$	$\frac{14}{9}$	$\frac{3}{2}$	$\frac{2}{7}$
$\frac{4}{15}$	$\frac{4}{21}$	$\frac{13}{56}$	$\frac{25}{12}$	$\frac{7}{36}$
$\frac{1}{2}$	$\frac{32}{15}$	$\frac{2}{9}$	$\frac{13}{24}$	$\frac{17}{28}$
$\frac{41}{18}$	$\frac{19}{20}$	$\frac{47}{56}$	$\frac{36}{35}$	$\frac{65}{36}$
$\frac{17}{18}$	$\frac{13}{12}$	$\frac{1}{12}$	$\frac{7}{45}$	$\frac{59}{18}$

Page 37

$\frac{19}{6}$	$\frac{37}{21}$	$\frac{11}{9}$	$\frac{11}{28}$	$\frac{1}{3}$
$\frac{3}{7}$	$\frac{7}{10}$	$\frac{17}{63}$	$\frac{7}{8}$	$\frac{8}{63}$
$\frac{1}{6}$	$\frac{7}{8}$	$\frac{56}{45}$	$\frac{23}{63}$	$\frac{3}{7}$
$\frac{2}{15}$	$\frac{5}{6}$	$\frac{47}{14}$	$\frac{9}{14}$	$\frac{7}{3}$
$\frac{1}{2}$	$\frac{47}{18}$	$\frac{1}{12}$	$\frac{47}{40}$	$\frac{13}{40}$

Page 38

$\frac{13}{45}$	$\frac{27}{10}$	$\frac{25}{36}$	$\frac{79}{18}$	$\frac{47}{21}$
$\frac{17}{63}$	$\frac{10}{63}$	$\frac{12}{35}$	$\frac{11}{15}$	$\frac{2}{15}$
$\frac{51}{56}$	$\frac{1}{18}$	$\frac{4}{63}$	$\frac{37}{72}$	$\frac{2}{15}$
$\frac{16}{35}$	$\frac{4}{21}$	$\frac{38}{35}$	$\frac{13}{56}$	$\frac{37}{14}$
$\frac{1}{8}$	$\frac{9}{56}$	$\frac{17}{21}$	$\frac{11}{28}$	$\frac{5}{12}$

Page 39

$\frac{31}{8}$	$\frac{21}{40}$	1	$\frac{1}{45}$	$\frac{5}{12}$
$\frac{13}{12}$	$\frac{11}{24}$	2	$\frac{21}{10}$	$\frac{13}{18}$
$\frac{31}{10}$	$\frac{17}{18}$	$\frac{17}{15}$	$\frac{31}{20}$	$\frac{1}{6}$
$\frac{13}{40}$	$\frac{23}{24}$	$\frac{9}{28}$	$\frac{3}{20}$	$\frac{31}{24}$
$\frac{19}{45}$	$\frac{1}{9}$	$\frac{23}{9}$	$\frac{59}{18}$	$\frac{23}{12}$

Page 40

$\frac{11}{35}$	$\frac{17}{6}$	$\frac{11}{12}$	$\frac{20}{63}$	$\frac{13}{12}$
$\frac{13}{15}$	$\frac{7}{36}$	$\frac{33}{10}$	$\frac{11}{8}$	$\frac{51}{56}$
$\frac{1}{5}$	$\frac{2}{7}$	$\frac{13}{24}$	$\frac{29}{20}$	$\frac{43}{35}$
$\frac{49}{36}$	$\frac{8}{45}$	$\frac{23}{14}$	$\frac{2}{15}$	$\frac{3}{35}$
$\frac{31}{10}$	$\frac{1}{5}$	$\frac{17}{40}$	$\frac{49}{45}$	$\frac{8}{15}$

Page 41

$\frac{1}{40}$	$\frac{7}{8}$	$\frac{12}{35}$	$\frac{19}{40}$	$\frac{5}{12}$
$\frac{7}{5}$	$\frac{5}{8}$	$\frac{38}{63}$	$\frac{2}{3}$	$\frac{46}{35}$
$\frac{13}{6}$	$\frac{25}{18}$	$\frac{8}{45}$	$\frac{11}{6}$	$\frac{23}{24}$
$\frac{2}{3}$	$\frac{2}{45}$	$\frac{41}{45}$	$\frac{41}{40}$	$\frac{1}{4}$
$\frac{19}{12}$	$\frac{5}{14}$	$\frac{31}{20}$	$\frac{41}{21}$	$\frac{31}{63}$

Page 42

$\frac{1}{7}$	$\frac{36}{35}$	$\frac{1}{5}$	$\frac{7}{4}$	$\frac{4}{7}$
$\frac{7}{20}$	$\frac{23}{36}$	$\frac{1}{6}$	$\frac{11}{30}$	$\frac{1}{18}$
$\frac{2}{3}$	$\frac{26}{63}$	2	$\frac{3}{4}$	$\frac{21}{20}$
$\frac{39}{10}$	$\frac{19}{15}$	$\frac{27}{20}$	$\frac{11}{24}$	$\frac{34}{35}$
$\frac{40}{63}$	$\frac{8}{63}$	$\frac{4}{35}$	$\frac{46}{35}$	$\frac{1}{3}$

Page 43

$\frac{1}{40}$	$\frac{59}{36}$	$\frac{58}{45}$	$\frac{19}{21}$	$\frac{31}{36}$
$\frac{1}{15}$	$\frac{23}{28}$	$\frac{11}{12}$	$\frac{11}{45}$	$\frac{55}{72}$
$\frac{1}{21}$	$\frac{11}{36}$	$\frac{67}{18}$	$\frac{7}{72}$	$\frac{51}{28}$
$\frac{2}{63}$	$\frac{41}{45}$	$\frac{22}{35}$	$\frac{1}{3}$	$\frac{1}{28}$
$\frac{2}{35}$	$\frac{23}{12}$	$\frac{9}{14}$	$\frac{3}{4}$	$\frac{17}{63}$

Page 44

$\frac{5}{18}$	$\frac{37}{40}$	$\frac{4}{7}$	$\frac{23}{30}$	$\frac{33}{14}$
$\frac{5}{21}$	$\frac{19}{9}$	$\frac{17}{14}$	$\frac{58}{45}$	$\frac{1}{24}$
$\frac{61}{36}$	$\frac{1}{8}$	$\frac{9}{28}$	$\frac{11}{42}$	$\frac{1}{20}$
$\frac{2}{3}$	$\frac{1}{12}$	$\frac{11}{12}$	$\frac{27}{56}$	$\frac{17}{15}$
$\frac{3}{8}$	$\frac{3}{7}$	$\frac{58}{63}$	$\frac{3}{4}$	$\frac{58}{35}$

Page 45

$\frac{46}{21}$	$\frac{65}{63}$	$\frac{41}{72}$	$\frac{5}{18}$	$\frac{2}{5}$
$\frac{19}{36}$	$\frac{31}{30}$	$\frac{1}{2}$	$\frac{5}{8}$	$\frac{19}{42}$
$\frac{41}{42}$	$\frac{2}{5}$	$\frac{71}{18}$	$\frac{23}{10}$	$\frac{2}{5}$
$\frac{9}{8}$	$\frac{16}{21}$	$\frac{44}{45}$	$\frac{19}{9}$	$\frac{1}{12}$
$\frac{5}{42}$	$\frac{23}{10}$	$\frac{23}{45}$	$\frac{33}{18}$	$\frac{5}{6}$

Page 46

$\frac{5}{21}$	$\frac{2}{3}$	$\frac{3}{2}$	$\frac{4}{9}$	$\frac{55}{14}$
$\frac{35}{36}$	$\frac{23}{10}$	$\frac{7}{12}$	$\frac{31}{21}$	$\frac{8}{21}$
$\frac{21}{20}$	$\frac{13}{12}$	$\frac{10}{9}$	$\frac{24}{35}$	$\frac{29}{56}$
$\frac{13}{28}$	$\frac{4}{15}$	$\frac{11}{8}$	$\frac{41}{72}$	$\frac{47}{72}$
$\frac{5}{6}$	$\frac{57}{56}$	$\frac{1}{10}$	$\frac{29}{63}$	$\frac{5}{63}$

Page 47

$\frac{22}{15}$	$\frac{55}{72}$	$\frac{1}{20}$	$\frac{1}{5}$	$\frac{29}{21}$
$\frac{27}{8}$	$\frac{17}{10}$	$\frac{25}{24}$	$\frac{3}{28}$	$\frac{11}{12}$
$\frac{13}{28}$	$\frac{8}{9}$	$\frac{13}{72}$	$\frac{8}{7}$	$\frac{38}{63}$
$\frac{1}{42}$	$\frac{37}{28}$	$\frac{1}{9}$	$\frac{33}{40}$	$\frac{31}{10}$
$\frac{31}{28}$	$\frac{5}{21}$	$\frac{13}{18}$	$\frac{1}{24}$	$\frac{7}{12}$

Page 48

$\frac{19}{10}$	$\frac{10}{63}$	$\frac{15}{4}$	$\frac{31}{42}$	$\frac{19}{18}$
$\frac{25}{21}$	$\frac{1}{72}$	$\frac{2}{63}$	$\frac{1}{20}$	$\frac{11}{10}$
$\frac{13}{6}$	$\frac{2}{5}$	$\frac{13}{63}$	$\frac{1}{18}$	$\frac{1}{8}$
$\frac{23}{45}$	$\frac{11}{14}$	$\frac{23}{35}$	$\frac{37}{24}$	$\frac{15}{8}$
$\frac{21}{20}$	$\frac{41}{24}$	$\frac{37}{30}$	$\frac{2}{7}$	$\frac{23}{56}$

Page 49

$\frac{29}{30}$	$\frac{5}{42}$	$\frac{23}{20}$	$\frac{36}{35}$	$\frac{2}{3}$
2	$\frac{2}{5}$	$\frac{53}{24}$	$\frac{11}{24}$	$\frac{29}{24}$
$\frac{11}{4}$	$\frac{5}{14}$	$\frac{13}{28}$	1	$\frac{1}{9}$
$\frac{26}{45}$	$\frac{7}{6}$	$\frac{19}{72}$	$\frac{19}{9}$	$\frac{14}{9}$
$\frac{41}{14}$	$\frac{47}{18}$	$\frac{2}{3}$	$\frac{6}{5}$	$\frac{14}{15}$

Page 50

$\frac{5}{6}$	$\frac{34}{35}$	$\frac{43}{30}$	$\frac{5}{14}$	$\frac{29}{40}$
$\frac{51}{40}$	$\frac{26}{63}$	$\frac{17}{30}$	$\frac{11}{21}$	$\frac{19}{18}$
$\frac{5}{6}$	$\frac{11}{30}$	$\frac{18}{35}$	$\frac{1}{7}$	$\frac{1}{5}$
$\frac{1}{9}$	$\frac{43}{21}$	$\frac{3}{56}$	$\frac{33}{20}$	$\frac{20}{21}$
$\frac{20}{9}$	2	$\frac{31}{42}$	$\frac{13}{24}$	$\frac{41}{14}$

Page 51

$\frac{7}{18}$	$\frac{5}{6}$	$\frac{5}{63}$	$\frac{17}{40}$	$\frac{17}{20}$
$\frac{53}{14}$	$\frac{27}{40}$	$\frac{17}{35}$	$\frac{11}{72}$	$\frac{19}{14}$
$\frac{2}{7}$	$\frac{3}{10}$	$\frac{9}{4}$	$\frac{29}{21}$	$\frac{3}{4}$
$\frac{3}{7}$	$\frac{33}{35}$	$\frac{47}{18}$	$\frac{20}{9}$	$\frac{13}{40}$
$\frac{2}{63}$	$\frac{5}{63}$	$\frac{1}{24}$	$\frac{18}{35}$	$\frac{7}{6}$

Page 52

$\frac{7}{24}$	$\frac{18}{35}$	$\frac{1}{4}$	$\frac{2}{5}$	$\frac{9}{14}$
$\frac{1}{4}$	$\frac{4}{35}$	$\frac{26}{45}$	$\frac{6}{35}$	$\frac{16}{35}$
$\frac{21}{40}$	$\frac{41}{56}$	$\frac{5}{12}$	$\frac{29}{28}$	$\frac{13}{21}$
$\frac{5}{4}$	4	$\frac{2}{3}$	$\frac{37}{72}$	$\frac{23}{40}$
$\frac{1}{30}$	$\frac{47}{36}$	$\frac{1}{8}$	$\frac{17}{42}$	$\frac{19}{15}$

Page 53

$\frac{45}{14}$	$\frac{18}{35}$	$\frac{11}{56}$	$\frac{8}{45}$	$\frac{11}{35}$
$\frac{5}{6}$	$\frac{47}{28}$	$\frac{25}{72}$	$\frac{17}{21}$	$\frac{53}{45}$
$\frac{50}{21}$	$\frac{13}{10}$	$\frac{19}{72}$	$\frac{1}{10}$	$\frac{11}{8}$
$\frac{16}{15}$	$\frac{5}{12}$	$\frac{31}{28}$	$\frac{10}{21}$	$\frac{1}{10}$
$\frac{9}{14}$	$\frac{11}{6}$	$\frac{53}{21}$	$\frac{1}{9}$	$\frac{31}{35}$

Page 54

$\frac{31}{30}$	$\frac{19}{20}$	$\frac{33}{14}$	$\frac{1}{18}$	$\frac{61}{36}$
$\frac{3}{4}$	$\frac{11}{45}$	$\frac{3}{5}$	$\frac{17}{40}$	$\frac{17}{28}$
$\frac{21}{10}$	$\frac{5}{8}$	$\frac{32}{35}$	$\frac{25}{36}$	$\frac{48}{35}$
$\frac{11}{14}$	$\frac{31}{21}$	$\frac{19}{56}$	$\frac{1}{63}$	$\frac{31}{72}$
$\frac{26}{21}$	$\frac{49}{24}$	$\frac{32}{21}$	$\frac{11}{18}$	$\frac{1}{3}$

Page 55

$\frac{29}{15}$	$\frac{43}{28}$	$\frac{21}{20}$	$\frac{23}{35}$	$\frac{4}{5}$
$\frac{13}{12}$	$\frac{2}{9}$	$\frac{1}{9}$	$\frac{6}{7}$	$\frac{19}{15}$
$\frac{7}{45}$	$\frac{7}{15}$	$\frac{17}{20}$	$\frac{3}{35}$	$\frac{33}{40}$
$\frac{31}{36}$	$\frac{11}{20}$	$\frac{17}{56}$	$\frac{19}{18}$	$\frac{31}{45}$
$\frac{6}{7}$	$\frac{19}{24}$	$\frac{19}{12}$	$\frac{17}{12}$	$\frac{40}{21}$

Page 56

$\frac{2}{63}$	$\frac{1}{15}$	$\frac{13}{18}$	$\frac{29}{12}$	$\frac{9}{28}$
$\frac{19}{40}$	$\frac{41}{40}$	$\frac{8}{63}$	$\frac{33}{35}$	$\frac{7}{20}$
$\frac{74}{63}$	$\frac{13}{28}$	$\frac{19}{6}$	$\frac{3}{5}$	$\frac{11}{35}$
$\frac{5}{18}$	$\frac{29}{24}$	$\frac{11}{21}$	$\frac{53}{45}$	$\frac{28}{15}$
$\frac{17}{15}$	$\frac{31}{28}$	$\frac{25}{42}$	$\frac{9}{35}$	$\frac{1}{3}$

Page 57

$\frac{5}{6}$	$\frac{37}{10}$	$\frac{38}{35}$	$\frac{14}{15}$	$\frac{41}{45}$
$\frac{7}{24}$	$\frac{19}{72}$	$\frac{1}{5}$	$\frac{2}{3}$	$\frac{5}{72}$
$\frac{47}{36}$	$\frac{47}{40}$	$\frac{23}{28}$	2	$\frac{8}{15}$
$\frac{7}{10}$	$\frac{3}{35}$	$\frac{13}{42}$	$\frac{5}{3}$	$\frac{19}{28}$
$\frac{13}{63}$	$\frac{6}{35}$	$\frac{14}{9}$	$\frac{1}{7}$	$\frac{5}{4}$

Part 3 Answers:

Page 59

$\frac{24}{35}$	$\frac{7}{12}$	$\frac{7}{32}$	$\frac{16}{21}$	$\frac{4}{15}$
$\frac{3}{28}$	$\frac{3}{16}$	$\frac{49}{25}$	$\frac{36}{35}$	$\frac{9}{20}$
$\frac{1}{4}$	$\frac{9}{10}$	$\frac{49}{24}$	$\frac{1}{14}$	$\frac{21}{16}$
$\frac{64}{27}$	$\frac{15}{16}$	$\frac{7}{12}$	$\frac{4}{45}$	$\frac{20}{3}$
$\frac{7}{64}$	$\frac{1}{15}$	$\frac{1}{2}$	$\frac{16}{27}$	$\frac{4}{3}$

Page 60

$\frac{16}{27}$	$\frac{4}{5}$	$\frac{1}{48}$	$\frac{3}{4}$	$\frac{9}{4}$
$\frac{81}{35}$	$\frac{25}{16}$	$\frac{14}{45}$	$\frac{5}{9}$	$\frac{48}{35}$
$\frac{81}{20}$	$\frac{27}{56}$	$\frac{1}{36}$	$\frac{8}{63}$	$\frac{35}{24}$
$\frac{16}{21}$	$\frac{4}{63}$	$\frac{7}{3}$	$\frac{1}{36}$	$\frac{9}{20}$
$\frac{2}{21}$	$\frac{21}{10}$	$\frac{5}{12}$	$\frac{1}{45}$	$\frac{45}{64}$

Page 61

$\frac{3}{20}$	$\frac{32}{15}$	$\frac{7}{6}$	$\frac{7}{5}$	$\frac{6}{7}$
$\frac{56}{9}$	$\frac{35}{6}$	$\frac{5}{4}$	$\frac{27}{14}$	$\frac{36}{35}$
$\frac{12}{49}$	$\frac{3}{35}$	$\frac{1}{45}$	$\frac{7}{5}$	$\frac{20}{9}$
$\frac{7}{20}$	$\frac{20}{27}$	$\frac{8}{25}$	$\frac{6}{35}$	$\frac{35}{24}$
$\frac{16}{21}$	$\frac{21}{5}$	$\frac{8}{27}$	$\frac{4}{27}$	$\frac{8}{63}$

Page 62

$\frac{49}{32}$	$\frac{9}{49}$	$\frac{9}{16}$	$\frac{7}{15}$	$\frac{1}{3}$
$\frac{35}{72}$	$\frac{72}{49}$	$\frac{63}{20}$	$\frac{1}{4}$	$\frac{7}{12}$
$\frac{7}{6}$	$\frac{5}{12}$	$\frac{8}{63}$	$\frac{25}{18}$	$\frac{81}{56}$
$\frac{5}{2}$	$\frac{1}{4}$	$\frac{5}{4}$	$\frac{81}{8}$	$\frac{63}{25}$
$\frac{1}{4}$	$\frac{35}{12}$	$\frac{49}{16}$	$\frac{20}{21}$	$\frac{15}{64}$

Page 63

$\frac{3}{4}$	$\frac{15}{28}$	$\frac{35}{72}$	$\frac{9}{28}$	$\frac{7}{27}$
$\frac{5}{2}$	$\frac{12}{25}$	$\frac{45}{56}$	$\frac{2}{21}$	$\frac{25}{36}$
$\frac{2}{9}$	$\frac{2}{15}$	$\frac{5}{8}$	$\frac{25}{36}$	$\frac{1}{8}$
$\frac{7}{4}$	$\frac{2}{3}$	$\frac{1}{5}$	$\frac{2}{9}$	$\frac{21}{64}$
$\frac{5}{7}$	$\frac{25}{36}$	$\frac{15}{32}$	$\frac{9}{4}$	$\frac{5}{56}$

Page 64

$\frac{1}{32}$	$\frac{1}{18}$	$\frac{45}{64}$	$\frac{5}{36}$	$\frac{27}{14}$
$\frac{35}{48}$	$\frac{9}{49}$	$\frac{1}{2}$	$\frac{25}{16}$	$\frac{16}{35}$
$\frac{8}{7}$	$\frac{8}{21}$	$\frac{3}{4}$	$\frac{45}{64}$	$\frac{24}{35}$
$\frac{15}{64}$	$\frac{8}{49}$	$\frac{25}{8}$	$\frac{24}{35}$	$\frac{8}{35}$
$\frac{32}{27}$	$\frac{5}{27}$	$\frac{21}{8}$	$\frac{32}{35}$	$\frac{64}{35}$

Practice Adding, Subtracting, Multiplying, and Dividing Fractions Workbook

Page 65

$$\frac{5}{12} \qquad \frac{8}{45} \qquad \frac{27}{64} \qquad \frac{21}{10} \qquad \frac{45}{32}$$
$$\frac{1}{5} \qquad \frac{5}{7} \qquad \frac{3}{10} \qquad \frac{5}{54} \qquad \frac{3}{10}$$
$$\frac{15}{49} \qquad \frac{1}{8} \qquad \frac{9}{4} \qquad \frac{6}{7} \qquad \frac{20}{21}$$
$$\frac{49}{81} \qquad \frac{27}{10} \qquad \frac{49}{12} \qquad \frac{1}{40} \qquad \frac{7}{12}$$
$$\frac{56}{15} \qquad \frac{18}{35} \qquad \frac{45}{64} \qquad \frac{9}{28} \qquad \frac{7}{5}$$

Page 66

$$\frac{8}{15} \qquad \frac{5}{18} \qquad \frac{5}{63} \qquad \frac{5}{54} \qquad \frac{7}{5}$$
$$\frac{7}{12} \qquad \frac{5}{48} \qquad \frac{63}{16} \qquad \frac{3}{20} \qquad \frac{21}{8}$$
$$\frac{16}{35} \qquad \frac{18}{49} \qquad \frac{32}{45} \qquad \frac{9}{7} \qquad \frac{16}{15}$$
$$\frac{3}{20} \qquad \frac{24}{49} \qquad \frac{3}{4} \qquad \frac{28}{45} \qquad \frac{3}{2}$$
$$\frac{1}{15} \qquad \frac{1}{2} \qquad \frac{3}{5} \qquad \frac{49}{32} \qquad \frac{5}{27}$$

Page 67

$$\frac{7}{15} \qquad \frac{16}{25} \qquad \frac{14}{9} \qquad \frac{1}{7} \qquad \frac{2}{35}$$
$$\frac{2}{3} \qquad \frac{21}{8} \qquad \frac{15}{4} \qquad \frac{7}{20} \qquad \frac{1}{8}$$
$$\frac{15}{14} \qquad \frac{28}{5} \qquad \frac{1}{14} \qquad \frac{48}{35} \qquad \frac{1}{5}$$
$$\frac{6}{5} \qquad \frac{27}{56} \qquad \frac{45}{8} \qquad \frac{7}{3} \qquad \frac{9}{40}$$
$$\frac{10}{3} \qquad \frac{7}{3} \qquad \frac{1}{3} \qquad \frac{81}{20} \qquad \frac{16}{49}$$

Page 68

$$\frac{6}{49} \qquad \frac{36}{35} \qquad \frac{1}{8} \qquad \frac{4}{3} \qquad \frac{21}{4}$$
$$\frac{5}{3} \qquad \frac{7}{27} \qquad \frac{35}{6} \qquad \frac{5}{24} \qquad \frac{7}{4}$$
$$\frac{25}{24} \qquad \frac{25}{81} \qquad \frac{15}{32} \qquad \frac{1}{10} \qquad \frac{1}{10}$$
$$\frac{7}{18} \qquad \frac{5}{7} \qquad \frac{5}{9} \qquad \frac{7}{27} \qquad \frac{15}{8}$$
$$\frac{27}{64} \qquad \frac{10}{9} \qquad \frac{3}{7} \qquad \frac{35}{54} \qquad \frac{1}{3}$$

Page 69

$$\frac{8}{27} \qquad \frac{4}{45} \qquad \frac{4}{5} \qquad \frac{10}{9} \qquad \frac{35}{72}$$
$$\frac{1}{6} \qquad \frac{25}{14} \qquad \frac{8}{9} \qquad \frac{45}{28} \qquad \frac{5}{3}$$
$$\frac{4}{21} \qquad \frac{24}{25} \qquad \frac{48}{49} \qquad \frac{1}{63} \qquad \frac{4}{21}$$
$$\frac{7}{36} \qquad \frac{49}{72} \qquad \frac{5}{7} \qquad \frac{9}{35} \qquad \frac{63}{10}$$
$$\frac{1}{18} \qquad \frac{9}{4} \qquad \frac{25}{42} \qquad \frac{25}{18} \qquad \frac{7}{2}$$

Page 70

$$\frac{3}{4} \qquad \frac{12}{35} \qquad \frac{7}{24} \qquad \frac{7}{8} \qquad \frac{9}{40}$$
$$\frac{32}{21} \qquad \frac{7}{5} \qquad \frac{7}{45} \qquad \frac{8}{3} \qquad \frac{42}{25}$$
$$\frac{1}{4} \qquad \frac{16}{15} \qquad \frac{9}{64} \qquad \frac{9}{14} \qquad \frac{7}{5}$$
$$\frac{5}{54} \qquad \frac{35}{12} \qquad \frac{1}{81} \qquad \frac{18}{49} \qquad \frac{2}{3}$$
$$\frac{49}{36} \qquad \frac{5}{2} \qquad \frac{49}{24} \qquad \frac{3}{10} \qquad \frac{4}{21}$$

Page 71

$$\frac{20}{27} \qquad \frac{1}{2} \qquad \frac{18}{49} \qquad \frac{15}{28} \qquad \frac{9}{28}$$
$$\frac{8}{5} \qquad \frac{35}{16} \qquad \frac{3}{7} \qquad \frac{21}{20} \qquad \frac{64}{15}$$
$$\frac{2}{25} \qquad \frac{4}{5} \qquad \frac{9}{7} \qquad \frac{27}{8} \qquad \frac{7}{2}$$
$$\frac{7}{4} \qquad \frac{8}{3} \qquad \frac{5}{56} \qquad \frac{40}{27} \qquad \frac{3}{8}$$
$$\frac{1}{27} \qquad \frac{81}{16} \qquad \frac{81}{14} \qquad \frac{5}{6} \qquad \frac{5}{14}$$

Page 72

$$\frac{1}{15} \qquad \frac{1}{9} \qquad \frac{28}{15} \qquad \frac{9}{14} \qquad \frac{5}{9}$$
$$\frac{7}{15} \qquad \frac{4}{27} \qquad \frac{5}{36} \qquad \frac{1}{24} \qquad \frac{48}{25}$$
$$\frac{7}{18} \qquad \frac{7}{5} \qquad \frac{49}{12} \qquad \frac{4}{3} \qquad \frac{14}{9}$$
$$\frac{8}{21} \qquad \frac{8}{25} \qquad \frac{35}{32} \qquad \frac{5}{6} \qquad \frac{5}{6}$$
$$\frac{7}{3} \qquad \frac{40}{21} \qquad \frac{27}{16} \qquad \frac{4}{7} \qquad \frac{1}{2}$$

Page 73

$\frac{2}{21}$	$\frac{5}{8}$	$\frac{14}{3}$	$\frac{21}{20}$	$\frac{3}{4}$
$\frac{27}{25}$	$\frac{49}{8}$	$\frac{63}{20}$	$\frac{3}{5}$	$\frac{5}{14}$
$\frac{64}{45}$	$\frac{25}{6}$	$\frac{6}{35}$	$\frac{1}{6}$	$\frac{6}{5}$
$\frac{1}{2}$	$\frac{1}{10}$	$\frac{56}{45}$	$\frac{3}{14}$	$\frac{3}{49}$
$\frac{1}{15}$	$\frac{4}{45}$	$\frac{28}{25}$	$\frac{2}{15}$	$\frac{1}{12}$

Page 74

$\frac{35}{16}$	$\frac{1}{27}$	$\frac{25}{42}$	$\frac{1}{2}$	$\frac{3}{7}$
$\frac{7}{16}$	$\frac{7}{9}$	$\frac{16}{81}$	$\frac{7}{18}$	$\frac{36}{25}$
$\frac{7}{9}$	$\frac{5}{16}$	$\frac{16}{81}$	$\frac{24}{5}$	$\frac{1}{2}$
$\frac{10}{3}$	$\frac{1}{9}$	$\frac{7}{27}$	$\frac{5}{28}$	$\frac{35}{18}$
$\frac{9}{5}$	$\frac{3}{8}$	$\frac{9}{28}$	$\frac{16}{15}$	$\frac{40}{21}$

Page 75

$\frac{35}{54}$	$\frac{63}{32}$	$\frac{4}{35}$	$\frac{27}{7}$	$\frac{40}{9}$
$\frac{45}{16}$	$\frac{81}{8}$	$\frac{1}{28}$	$\frac{7}{81}$	$\frac{6}{5}$
$\frac{27}{25}$	$\frac{1}{3}$	$\frac{64}{45}$	$\frac{25}{36}$	$\frac{1}{18}$
$\frac{3}{25}$	$\frac{8}{3}$	$\frac{2}{7}$	$\frac{3}{35}$	$\frac{21}{10}$
$\frac{27}{28}$	$\frac{2}{7}$	$\frac{81}{28}$	$\frac{2}{3}$	$\frac{3}{7}$

Page 76

$\frac{7}{10}$	$\frac{32}{45}$	$\frac{9}{5}$	$\frac{15}{8}$	$\frac{8}{25}$
$\frac{63}{8}$	$\frac{16}{63}$	$\frac{24}{25}$	$\frac{1}{12}$	$\frac{4}{21}$
$\frac{20}{27}$	$\frac{25}{24}$	$\frac{7}{5}$	$\frac{2}{3}$	$\frac{27}{20}$
$\frac{25}{21}$	$\frac{15}{14}$	$\frac{1}{18}$	$\frac{3}{8}$	$\frac{25}{6}$
$\frac{16}{45}$	$\frac{63}{64}$	$\frac{24}{35}$	$\frac{3}{16}$	$\frac{7}{8}$

Page 77

$\frac{35}{12}$	$\frac{35}{9}$	$\frac{5}{42}$	$\frac{21}{8}$	$\frac{36}{7}$
$\frac{14}{5}$	$\frac{7}{3}$	$\frac{1}{12}$	$\frac{45}{16}$	$\frac{63}{25}$
$\frac{1}{3}$	$\frac{5}{27}$	$\frac{9}{25}$	$\frac{5}{24}$	$\frac{32}{15}$
$\frac{2}{27}$	$\frac{1}{7}$	$\frac{4}{21}$	$\frac{16}{25}$	$\frac{8}{25}$
$\frac{5}{12}$	$\frac{7}{10}$	$\frac{27}{40}$	$\frac{3}{35}$	$\frac{49}{10}$

Page 78

$\frac{2}{7}$	$\frac{3}{2}$	$\frac{12}{25}$	$\frac{7}{24}$	$\frac{1}{6}$
$\frac{4}{63}$	$\frac{25}{36}$	$\frac{63}{16}$	$\frac{63}{16}$	$\frac{14}{27}$
$\frac{2}{9}$	$\frac{5}{16}$	$\frac{8}{35}$	$\frac{35}{24}$	$\frac{1}{3}$
$\frac{5}{9}$	$\frac{2}{15}$	$\frac{1}{12}$	$\frac{25}{12}$	$\frac{15}{28}$
$\frac{7}{15}$	$\frac{7}{8}$	$\frac{4}{15}$	$\frac{1}{8}$	$\frac{45}{32}$

Page 79

$\frac{2}{35}$	$\frac{7}{2}$	$\frac{4}{21}$	$\frac{35}{9}$	$\frac{5}{28}$
$\frac{2}{3}$	$\frac{27}{14}$	$\frac{9}{28}$	$\frac{1}{4}$	$\frac{7}{32}$
$\frac{6}{5}$	$\frac{9}{7}$	$\frac{14}{5}$	$\frac{16}{45}$	$\frac{4}{35}$
$\frac{20}{9}$	$\frac{49}{10}$	$\frac{2}{27}$	$\frac{63}{10}$	$\frac{1}{2}$
$\frac{7}{2}$	$\frac{9}{40}$	$\frac{9}{10}$	$\frac{1}{3}$	$\frac{3}{64}$

Page 80

$\frac{27}{35}$	$\frac{81}{16}$	$\frac{1}{6}$	$\frac{63}{8}$	$\frac{25}{28}$
$\frac{5}{2}$	$\frac{2}{49}$	$\frac{9}{10}$	$\frac{14}{27}$	$\frac{35}{16}$
$\frac{12}{7}$	$\frac{5}{7}$	$\frac{1}{12}$	$\frac{7}{4}$	$\frac{4}{9}$
$\frac{3}{2}$	$\frac{1}{3}$	$\frac{1}{21}$	$\frac{3}{16}$	$\frac{14}{81}$
$\frac{1}{4}$	$\frac{1}{2}$	$\frac{18}{35}$	$\frac{20}{27}$	$\frac{40}{27}$

Page 81

$\frac{4}{15}$	$\frac{35}{12}$	$\frac{7}{8}$	$\frac{9}{4}$	$\frac{1}{3}$
$\frac{45}{28}$	$\frac{28}{45}$	$\frac{9}{4}$	$\frac{9}{10}$	$\frac{16}{63}$
$\frac{49}{6}$	$\frac{3}{28}$	$\frac{5}{2}$	$\frac{7}{27}$	$\frac{5}{2}$
$\frac{20}{27}$	$\frac{14}{9}$	$\frac{7}{27}$	$\frac{1}{6}$	$\frac{10}{9}$
$\frac{7}{48}$	$\frac{63}{8}$	$\frac{2}{3}$	$\frac{1}{15}$	$\frac{15}{64}$

Page 82

$\frac{9}{25}$	$\frac{18}{49}$	$\frac{5}{9}$	$\frac{25}{32}$	$\frac{32}{49}$
$\frac{14}{45}$	$\frac{9}{8}$	$\frac{3}{32}$	$\frac{25}{36}$	$\frac{6}{5}$
	$\frac{4}{9}$	$\frac{5}{16}$	$\frac{5}{42}$	$\frac{1}{18}$
	$\frac{9}{56}$	$\frac{1}{5}$	$\frac{14}{9}$	$\frac{1}{8}$
	$\frac{3}{2}$	$\frac{15}{28}$	$\frac{5}{16}$	$\frac{7}{6}$
$\frac{4}{1}$	$\frac{1}{24}$	$\frac{1}{5}$	$\frac{35}{9}$
$\frac{7}{8}$	$\frac{7}{5}$	$\frac{1}{28}$	$\frac{3}{4}$
$\frac{5}{2}$	$\frac{5}{8}$	$\frac{7}{24}$	$\frac{4}{15}$
$\frac{?}{3}$	$\frac{7}{20}$	$\frac{1}{36}$	$\frac{7}{12}$
	$\frac{1}{3}$	$\frac{1}{10}$	$\frac{81}{10}$

rs:

$\frac{1}{36}$	$\frac{2}{7}$	$\frac{56}{3}$
$\frac{8}{3}$	$\frac{21}{8}$	$\frac{18}{49}$
$\frac{2}{3}$	$\frac{3}{2}$	$\frac{28}{27}$
$\frac{54}{25}$	$\frac{2}{9}$	$\frac{21}{2}$
$\frac{63}{16}$	$\frac{35}{32}$	$\frac{1}{16}$

Page 86

$\frac{8}{63}$	$\frac{10}{3}$	$\frac{7}{4}$	$\frac{25}{27}$	$\frac{35}{12}$
$\frac{32}{21}$	$\frac{5}{24}$	$\frac{81}{8}$	$\frac{40}{27}$	$\frac{64}{63}$
$\frac{4}{21}$	$\frac{49}{24}$	$\frac{7}{8}$	$\frac{5}{42}$	$\frac{63}{20}$
$\frac{20}{63}$	$\frac{5}{4}$	$\frac{8}{15}$	$\frac{20}{7}$	$\frac{45}{56}$
$\frac{12}{49}$	$\frac{9}{20}$	$\frac{35}{6}$	$\frac{27}{16}$	$\frac{5}{14}$

Page 87

$\frac{28}{5}$	$\frac{9}{4}$	$\frac{1}{7}$	$\frac{14}{27}$	$\frac{27}{14}$
$\frac{45}{28}$	$\frac{7}{30}$	$\frac{5}{4}$	$\frac{5}{9}$	$\frac{14}{25}$
$\frac{1}{7}$	$\frac{5}{9}$	$\frac{63}{8}$	$\frac{27}{14}$	$\frac{16}{9}$
$\frac{27}{5}$	$\frac{3}{28}$	$\frac{1}{4}$	$\frac{8}{27}$	$\frac{25}{64}$
$\frac{9}{25}$	$\frac{35}{4}$	$\frac{3}{28}$	$\frac{54}{35}$	$\frac{5}{7}$

Page 88

$\frac{32}{7}$	$\frac{3}{7}$	$\frac{5}{42}$	$\frac{27}{14}$	$\frac{27}{10}$
$\frac{49}{30}$	$\frac{7}{8}$	$\frac{1}{6}$	$\frac{32}{7}$	$\frac{27}{7}$
$\frac{5}{14}$	$\frac{25}{49}$	$\frac{8}{5}$	$\frac{32}{9}$	$\frac{21}{64}$
$\frac{5}{14}$	$\frac{4}{5}$	$\frac{21}{25}$	$\frac{9}{2}$	$\frac{4}{27}$
$\frac{2}{9}$	$\frac{63}{16}$	$\frac{1}{3}$	$\frac{5}{9}$	$\frac{5}{32}$

Page 89

$\frac{3}{4}$	$\frac{3}{8}$	$\frac{12}{7}$	$\frac{3}{10}$	$\frac{3}{5}$
$\frac{63}{5}$	$\frac{4}{21}$	$\frac{49}{45}$	$\frac{9}{10}$	$\frac{5}{63}$
$\frac{35}{9}$	$\frac{27}{14}$	$\frac{7}{6}$	$\frac{24}{49}$	$\frac{18}{25}$
$\frac{28}{5}$	$\frac{2}{3}$	$\frac{5}{12}$	$\frac{15}{14}$	$\frac{21}{10}$
$\frac{72}{7}$	$\frac{9}{5}$	$\frac{25}{3}$	$\frac{5}{21}$	$\frac{1}{7}$

Page 90

7/9	49/48	3/7	10/9	8/49
15/4	1/8	6/7	36/25	40/7
3/7	63/32	16/27	14/3	4/27
7/2	15/8	49/4	49/30	16/21
1/2	14/9	5/9	4/3	35/36

Page 91

7/6	24/35	3/10	35/16	1/4
8/7	63/8	27/10	15/7	7/48
20/63	7/10	9/2	7/30	15/7
35/6	63/8	10/81	14/5	81/32
32/27	9/20	1/21	48/35	1/4

Page 92

16/5	12/7	54/49	2/9	5/6
32/25	9/40	18/5	56/3	7/48
3/2	3/2	25/64	18/7	27/56
56/27	9/5	21/25	4/35	64/21
18/49	14/3	10/7	5/36	7/8

Page 93

32/9	1/2	4/3	2/27	8/27
2/45	4/21	35/6	3/4	5/9
9/4	5/49	15/4	10/27	1/15
9/4	49/36	28/15	7/81	72/7
81/4	7/3	7/8	3/2	27/28

Page 94

54/49	35/18	3/35	12/7	27/10
8/15	36/7	20/63	7/20	35/32
8/3	35/9	1/2	7/8	49/45
8/25	28/15	18/7	35/36	27/20
9/2	32/3	1/14	2/3	1/2

Page 95

36/7	56/25	2/63	3/10	25/12
7/8	5/3	35/48	49/40	25/16
1/9	63/8	1/24	1/9	8/3
36/25	8/25	2/5	56/81	45/16
20/27	1/8	1/2	81/35	49/72

Page 96

35/12	21/20	25/24	49/48	5/18
7/4	7/3	3/28	21/20	28/81
48/49	1/3	9/35	56/3	35/9
35/24	32/25	45/49	32/63	3/7
8/63	2/3	3/5	35/3	2/5

Page 97

9/14	1/7	4/9	3/2	45/32
21/10	14/25	63/10	35/18	1/3
24/5	6/5	1/3	2/3	40/63
18/35	1/2	5/6	18/7	9/5
27/32	49/5	35/8	5/32	7/5

Page 98

$\frac{5}{4}$	$\frac{8}{21}$	$\frac{5}{27}$	$\frac{32}{9}$	$\frac{16}{45}$
$\frac{8}{9}$	$\frac{25}{54}$	$\frac{1}{3}$	$\frac{1}{4}$	$\frac{8}{5}$
$\frac{28}{15}$	$\frac{18}{7}$	$\frac{21}{16}$	$\frac{8}{63}$	$\frac{10}{9}$
$\frac{5}{24}$	$\frac{40}{21}$	$\frac{24}{5}$	$\frac{49}{36}$	$\frac{9}{20}$
$\frac{1}{14}$	$\frac{1}{6}$	$\frac{5}{2}$	$\frac{1}{2}$	$\frac{45}{56}$

Page 99

$\frac{63}{20}$	$\frac{63}{20}$	$\frac{27}{7}$	$\frac{40}{9}$	$\frac{7}{12}$
$\frac{7}{4}$	$\frac{9}{14}$	$\frac{3}{4}$	$\frac{16}{9}$	$\frac{1}{3}$
$\frac{54}{5}$	$\frac{35}{24}$	$\frac{5}{12}$	$\frac{12}{25}$	$\frac{2}{3}$
$\frac{9}{49}$	$\frac{27}{20}$	$\frac{35}{48}$	$\frac{9}{4}$	$\frac{28}{15}$
$\frac{27}{16}$	$\frac{12}{35}$	$\frac{18}{35}$	$\frac{14}{9}$	$\frac{25}{6}$

Page 100

$\frac{24}{35}$	$\frac{49}{10}$	$\frac{49}{12}$	$\frac{63}{20}$	$\frac{2}{3}$
$\frac{25}{8}$	$\frac{8}{3}$	$\frac{32}{9}$	$\frac{45}{49}$	$\frac{5}{18}$
$\frac{25}{24}$	$\frac{4}{7}$	$\frac{10}{63}$	$\frac{36}{25}$	$\frac{21}{4}$
$\frac{64}{7}$	$\frac{25}{8}$	$\frac{72}{49}$	$\frac{5}{7}$	$\frac{4}{9}$
$\frac{3}{4}$	$\frac{81}{10}$	$\frac{9}{10}$	$\frac{14}{5}$	$\frac{35}{32}$

Page 101

$\frac{54}{49}$	$\frac{21}{2}$	$\frac{45}{4}$	$\frac{32}{15}$	$\frac{36}{5}$
$\frac{27}{25}$	$\frac{64}{9}$	$\frac{8}{63}$	$\frac{1}{18}$	$\frac{35}{16}$
$\frac{25}{27}$	$\frac{1}{3}$	$\frac{25}{12}$	$\frac{5}{7}$	$\frac{63}{16}$
$\frac{1}{2}$	$\frac{35}{32}$	$\frac{54}{35}$	$\frac{7}{4}$	$\frac{4}{9}$
$\frac{2}{45}$	$\frac{9}{56}$	$\frac{15}{16}$	$\frac{24}{49}$	$\frac{9}{28}$

Page 102

$\frac{16}{15}$	$\frac{8}{35}$	$\frac{9}{35}$	$\frac{28}{3}$	$\frac{7}{5}$
$\frac{81}{4}$	$\frac{5}{42}$	$\frac{36}{5}$	$\frac{3}{14}$	$\frac{9}{16}$
$\frac{16}{5}$	$\frac{15}{8}$	$\frac{5}{6}$	$\frac{5}{14}$	$\frac{27}{32}$
$\frac{72}{35}$	$\frac{40}{21}$	$\frac{7}{2}$	$\frac{5}{63}$	$\frac{7}{3}$
$\frac{21}{64}$	$\frac{16}{7}$	$\frac{35}{8}$	$\frac{49}{30}$	$\frac{32}{7}$

Page 103

$\frac{21}{10}$	$\frac{14}{5}$	$\frac{49}{45}$	$\frac{5}{72}$	$\frac{7}{4}$
$\frac{28}{3}$	$\frac{1}{3}$	$\frac{2}{15}$	$\frac{48}{49}$	$\frac{5}{7}$
$\frac{9}{28}$	$\frac{36}{35}$	$\frac{14}{9}$	$\frac{1}{2}$	$\frac{35}{18}$
$\frac{7}{24}$	$\frac{9}{5}$	$\frac{16}{3}$	$\frac{5}{7}$	$\frac{9}{56}$
$\frac{9}{20}$	$\frac{81}{40}$	$\frac{15}{28}$	$\frac{3}{7}$	$\frac{15}{16}$

Page 104

$\frac{7}{5}$	$\frac{7}{24}$	$\frac{27}{16}$	$\frac{16}{9}$	$\frac{8}{21}$
$\frac{28}{15}$	$\frac{56}{15}$	$\frac{4}{63}$	$\frac{8}{15}$	$\frac{5}{4}$
$\frac{3}{4}$	$\frac{1}{8}$	$\frac{25}{18}$	$\frac{32}{9}$	$\frac{5}{28}$
$\frac{49}{12}$	$\frac{20}{9}$	$\frac{1}{8}$	$\frac{20}{63}$	$\frac{3}{10}$
$\frac{35}{12}$	$\frac{1}{2}$	$\frac{5}{21}$	$\frac{15}{16}$	$\frac{25}{42}$

Page 105

$\frac{1}{5}$	$\frac{35}{8}$	$\frac{32}{21}$	$\frac{30}{7}$	$\frac{7}{2}$
$\frac{16}{21}$	$\frac{5}{8}$	$\frac{35}{32}$	$\frac{12}{25}$	$\frac{4}{63}$
$\frac{36}{35}$	$\frac{32}{15}$	$\frac{2}{5}$	$\frac{10}{9}$	$\frac{15}{28}$
$\frac{1}{3}$	$\frac{3}{2}$	$\frac{3}{2}$	$\frac{28}{9}$	$\frac{36}{7}$
$\frac{21}{5}$	$\frac{1}{3}$	$\frac{21}{20}$	$\frac{16}{27}$	$\frac{36}{5}$

Page 106

$\frac{3}{56}$	$\frac{10}{9}$	$\frac{1}{3}$	$\frac{8}{15}$	$\frac{5}{54}$
$\frac{49}{18}$	$\frac{7}{15}$	$\frac{1}{3}$	$\frac{18}{49}$	$\frac{15}{16}$
$\frac{10}{7}$	$\frac{5}{28}$	$\frac{56}{27}$	$\frac{15}{16}$	$\frac{1}{4}$
$\frac{21}{8}$	$\frac{1}{4}$	$\frac{27}{2}$	$\frac{14}{5}$	$\frac{5}{42}$
$\frac{9}{32}$	$\frac{35}{4}$	$\frac{7}{3}$	$\frac{81}{56}$	$\frac{9}{35}$

Page 107

$\frac{25}{18}$	$\frac{16}{5}$	$\frac{28}{5}$	$\frac{8}{7}$	$\frac{5}{54}$
$\frac{3}{8}$	$\frac{7}{2}$	$\frac{1}{3}$	$\frac{16}{45}$	$\frac{4}{35}$
$\frac{9}{28}$	$\frac{9}{16}$	$\frac{56}{27}$	$\frac{9}{5}$	$\frac{25}{18}$
$\frac{14}{5}$	$\frac{81}{14}$	$\frac{4}{7}$	$\frac{5}{18}$	$\frac{5}{24}$
$\frac{4}{7}$	$\frac{7}{9}$	$\frac{7}{4}$	$\frac{64}{9}$	$\frac{16}{21}$

Page 108

$\frac{35}{18}$	$\frac{4}{15}$	$\frac{63}{40}$	$\frac{28}{3}$	$\frac{4}{9}$
$\frac{36}{49}$	$\frac{6}{5}$	$\frac{16}{21}$	$\frac{4}{9}$	$\frac{1}{2}$
$\frac{5}{3}$	$\frac{4}{3}$	$\frac{9}{7}$	$\frac{16}{7}$	$\frac{14}{45}$
$\frac{15}{14}$	$\frac{28}{5}$	$\frac{5}{8}$	$\frac{12}{5}$	$\frac{49}{16}$
$\frac{21}{10}$	$\frac{5}{27}$	$\frac{1}{3}$	$\frac{2}{7}$	$\frac{24}{5}$

Page 109

$\frac{10}{7}$	$\frac{28}{15}$	$\frac{15}{16}$	$\frac{54}{49}$	$\frac{1}{36}$
$\frac{10}{27}$	$\frac{7}{16}$	$\frac{36}{7}$	$\frac{8}{5}$	$\frac{4}{3}$
$\frac{3}{5}$	$\frac{9}{4}$	$\frac{1}{4}$	$\frac{1}{10}$	$\frac{10}{27}$
$\frac{2}{9}$	$\frac{36}{25}$	$\frac{40}{21}$	$\frac{5}{36}$	$\frac{4}{5}$
$\frac{28}{45}$	$\frac{9}{32}$	$\frac{35}{54}$	$\frac{25}{42}$	$\frac{21}{4}$

Made in the USA
Middletown, DE
24 June 2015